JUMPING
THE
QUEUE

Michelle Turman

ACHIEVING GREAT THINGS
BEFORE YOU'RE READY

MICHELLE A. TURMAN, M.A., CFRE

Praise for *Jumping the Queue* and Michelle A. Turman

A must-read for future female leaders who endeavor to leave a lasting impact. Turman shares stories of successes and failures to illustrate how both are necessary to learn and grow personally and professionally. Her candor is a breath of fresh air!

Jessica Rivelli,
Founder of the Working Women Foundation

An insightful, honest book filled with inspiration and wisdom for anyone entering the workforce. A roadmap for success, Michelle Turman's story demonstrates that you need not stand in line for the next opportunity. Ambition, drive, and taking a chance with your career are the keys to reaching your destination.

Rita Lowman,
Bank Executive, 2017/18 Chair of the Florida Bankers Association,
Author of From the Farm to the Boardroom: Leadership Lessons

Michelle Turman's book, Jumping the Queue is an upbeat breath of fresh air for ambitious women who are not interested in the traditional model of waiting ten or twenty years for the right opportunity. Written from her own experiences, Turman creates a path for women who want their lives to be adventurous, successful, fast-paced, and even a bit scary. She is honest, funny, and uses the power of story to share the key life decisions she made that led to opportunity and success. I highly recommend this book to any women who are ready to propel their lives forward.

Kari Saddler,
Founder of Daily Leadership Coaching

Young professional women thirsty for mentorship will benefit from Turman's authentic and inspirational story. She outlines the mindset, compass points, and steps necessary for success as your career evolves. A must-read for integrating your life and your career.

Michele Norris,
Founder, Navigen Leadership of Caring

As a millennial and the CEO of a multimillion-dollar ad agency, I know a thing or two about "jumping the queue," and I wish I had read this book sooner. It goes straight to the heart of how to recognize and avoid the detractors that hinder you from believing in yourself and achieving your true potential. If you seek to find purpose and achieve your big dreams, don't wait. This book is a must-read.

Lauren Davenport,
Founder of The Symphony Agency

This book resonated with me on many levels! Jumping the Queue confirms that defining what you want and believing in yourself are critical to achieving personal and professional goals. Through Turman's words and real-life examples, I'm inspired to create even bigger dreams and goals!

Lisa L. Demmi,
Keynote Speaker and Trainer

There is one thing wrong with this book: I wish it had been published when I was in my twenties. Everything Michelle writes resonates with me, now more than ever. I found motivation, inspiration, compassion, and sound advice among these pages. You couldn't ask for a better guide to see you through some of the toughest times in life. You'll be nodding in agreement through the whole read. Get this for your daughter, your sister, your wife, your friend, or anyone who needs that extra push to know she can do it.

Margaret Cardillo,
Award-winning author, screenwriter, and editor

Jumping the Queue is a riveting narrative about the power of believing in yourself. It's about trusting in your own process over "the" process. It's about learning to welcome uncertainty—to embrace it. It's about achieving the unlikely, not the impossible.

Miraj Patel,
Founder, Harness Innovative Fundraising Solutions

As a female entrepreneur whose path has been anything but straight, I can definitely relate, both personally and professionally, to the stories Michelle bravely shares in Jumping the Queue. An inspirational read for any woman who has loads of enthusiasm and passion for their big ideas but lacks the experience or mentorship needed to execute their goals. Proof that waiting until you are "ready" to get started is not always the best policy.

Krayl Funch,
Author of An Appealing Plan:
A Lifetime of Everyday Celebrations

Jumping the Queue goes directly to the heart of why the "contractor mindset" of millennials is the future of how our leaders think and work.

Trimeka Benjamin,
President & CEO of Swim Digital Group

This is a brilliant handbook and a source of great inspiration analyzing the position, psychology, and potential of women in contemporary business, based on Turman's own rich—and in many ways unique—work experience in multiple fields.

Of particular interest for those who know Michelle primarily as the curator/conservator of the Titanic artifacts and the youngest female diver to this historical wreck is the chapter devoted to her valiant and highly professional work during the first Titanic expedition of the new millennium.

Eugene Nesmeyanov,
Author of The Shipbuilding and Titanic researcher

Editorial Project Management: Front Rowe Seat Communications, karen@karenrowe.com

Cover Design: Shake Creative, ShakeTampa.com

Inside Layout: Ljiljana Pavkov

Printed in the United States of America

FIRST EDITION

ISBN: 978-1-5323-4905-8 (international trade paper edition)
ISBN: 978-1-5323-4906-5 (eBook)

Published by Catalyst Consulting Services, LLC

10 9 8 7 6 5 4 3 2 1

For Matthew and Nicholas

*"May your ascents always be greater
than your descents."*

—RALPH WHITE,
RMS TITANIC EXPLORER & DOCUMENTARIAN,
AND NATIONAL GEOGRAPHIC CINEMATOGRAPHER

Table of Contents

JUMPING
THE
QUEUE

Acknowledgments

Thanks to all the people I met over the years during my travels—some of whom I kept in touch, some of whom I put into this book, and some who challenged me in ways that strengthened my drive, purpose, and passion. Each of you, in some way, changed the trajectory of my life. Without you, I would not be here writing these words.

I am grateful to family and friends who have provided me with unconditional support; mentors who have offered guidance; employers who gave me the opportunity to sharpen my skills; and clients who entrusted me to be a catalyst for positive change for their for-profit or nonprofit organizations.

Finally, a thank you to Eric, Matthew, and Nicholas. You are the ones I travel with now. What a joyful and loving journey it is.

Introduction

When I was forty I got this crazy idea to leave my comfortable, well-paying job in order to start my own consulting business. As this idea became more real, I went to my see my boss. He was set to retire in a couple of years and I was being groomed to take over as CEO. Since I had been hired as part of his transition plan, I felt I owed him plenty of notice. In the interest of full transparency, I told him my plans.

"I feel a responsibility to tell you that I really don't think that I'm going to be moving forward with this role," I said. "I have decided to start my own business. I want to give you at least six months notice. After that, if you continue to need me, I would be happy to serve in a consultant capacity.

My boss was taken aback. "I'm retiring in a few years," he said. "You are the person I'm supposed to be handing the ball to." As our conversation concluded, he grudgingly said, "Well, I know you'll be really successful."

The next Monday, it became clear just how upset he was. He called me into his office and said, "You know, I was thinking a lot about what you said. It's probably better if you leave in the next month or so."

Suddenly, my timeline had shrunk.

One month.

My husband freaked out. "What are we going to do for money? Where are your clients going to come from?" He is in business development so it was a valid question, but I hadn't even thought about it. I had my network, after all. When I told him, he asked me what I *was* worried about. What I was worried about was that I had never started a business from scratch. Filing for the LLC, designing the logo, learning how to do the taxes and paperwork—it was all such a big deal.

Ultimately, I was forced to admit: I was not completely ready. Did this bother me?

Not one bit.

In fact, I had never been "ready" for many of the great things I have achieved in my professional and personal life. I had never felt content to wait for anything until I was ready. In hindsight, I realize that this attitude is similar to the mindset of today's younger professionals

We're all familiar with the stereotype. Gen X'ers and millennials are lazy and selfish. They are self-centered egomaniacs who would rather sit around taking selfies than putting in an honest day's work. But in reality, the biggest problem most young professionals face is that they are enthusiastic and have big ideas, but they lack the tools and experience to execute and implement their concepts. These qualities have been misjudged by society.

The main thing that I see with millennials and Gen X'ers is that they are simply *unwilling to wait*. If something does not seem to be working their way, they're not going to stick around. They learn their lesson, cut their losses, and move on to the next thing. In other words, millennials tend to be *impatient*. One of the challenges they face today is how to resolve their characteristic impatience when entering the working world.

Millennial and Gen X women are living in a time when career opportunities have never been better—if you want them, that is. This book is about seizing opportunities, achieving great things, and getting what you want from your life.

The first step toward getting what you want is *knowing* what you want. In order to do that, you have to put yourself out there and be vulnerable. That is a challenge for some women, especially if they're not confident, unsure about what they want, or don't feel "ready."

But I say being "ready" is overrated.

I wrote this book specifically to help young professional women discover what they want out of life, to embrace that impatience, and achieve great things—*before* they're ready.

In the past, most people accepted the necessity of "putting in the time." They would put in the work to get their degree, learn the ins and the outs of a position, stay in that position for a certain amount of time, and wait until there was a chance to move up to a better position. You had to hope that you would be in the right place when the next opportunity presented itself, waiting for your turn in a slow, steady queue.

Playing the waiting game to gain that experience, knowledge, and rapport is something millennials and Gen X'ers are not willing to do. If what they want doesn't happen within a certain amount of time, they move on to something different, or go create an opportunity that works for them and fits their lifestyle.

Jumping the Queue, is for young women who want to create their own opportunities, embrace their impatience, and achieve great things *before* they are ready. If you grew up having everything handed to you, then this book is not for you. If you had an idyllic family life, this book is not for you. If you have been, or continue to be, a follower and not a leader and have no interest in facilitating change, return this book and get a refund now.

However, if you have dreamed big, faltered, challenged the status quo, been the minority in a group, and have the tenacity to create your own destiny and to write your own rulebook, then read on.

***

Starting my own business was not the only thing I did before I was ready. Looking back, I could never have known that my decisions to "jump the queue" would lead me to become the youngest woman to dive the Titanic; or becoming the youngest female museum art director in Florida; or attain enough success in the nonprofit sector in order to start my own consulting company. As a result, my journey took me around the world, to the bottom of the ocean, to the top of the corporate ladder, and just about everywhere in between. It's a process and a mindset that I aim to pass on to millennial women in this book.

I do a lot of business with young professionals, particularly women. And far from the lazy, selfie-snapping narcissists that millennials are portrayed as, what I see are motivated women who are riding the waves of change instead of trying to swim against the current. These are young women who realize that the world is changing and that they must change with it.

This is not a book about women's rights, civil rights, or feminism. I feel fortunate, and carry much gratitude for those who have paved the way and allowed me to stand on their shoulders. The stories in this book are rooted in a time when there was opportunity, even if it was limited. Education was accessible to me, even if the means to afford it may not have been. Mentorship was readily available, even if it was mostly aligned with male counterparts. What will always be relevant is how men *and* women deal with stress and how it affects the body and mind. What will also be relevant is when—not how or why—women leaders will be equivalent in the boardroom, in pay, and in credibility.

The stories in this book deal with pulling back the veil of what it takes to be a *female* leader. I am not here to discuss whether or not biology plays a role in leadership, nor am I here to question the choices that other women have made. I am here to share my viewpoint, share my journey, the cost, the true meaning of success, and the impact that is still left to be made in the world, based on my experiences. My story isn't that of the vice president of a Fortune 500 company, a Supreme Court justice, or a secretary of state. But it is the story of what it means to become a leader as a woman, particularly in the world of business.

This will be a candid, unapologetic discussion of the road I've faced, complete with the trials, challenges, heartbreaks, and missteps I had along the way. When we read about those vice presidents, Supreme Court justices, and secretaries of state, such candidness is usually absent. We may not get the full story of the missteps, personal stories of choice, and compromises, as the personal risk of divulging such information is far greater in such cases.

Why do I share my pain, my disappointments, my joys, losses, and triumphs? Because when we know better, we do better. When I think about those who have had the greatest impact on my life, it is those who failed, succeeded, and failed again, and then shared their story who has made an impact on me. It shows that they possess an innate belief in themselves, a desire to maximize their God-given talents and the vulnerability to be humble.

The book is truly about sharing how extraordinary experiences can mold a woman's character at each stage in her life. This is about the challenges and trials that any young woman who aspires to be a leader should expect to face along her journey—and to overcome.

As the saying goes, "be the change you want to see in the world." This is why I write for you—with honesty, vulnerability, and as a facilitator of change for the next leader. You have the power to create your own opportunities. You have the power to create the world you want to live in.

Chapter 1

Overcoming Adversity

"Little girls with dreams become women with vision."

—Unknown

I recently had a conversation with two millennials who are on the board of a nonprofit. One was in the process of applying for a job within the team; the other was applying for a job out of state. Both of them told me, separately, that it would be the first time they had ever been on a job interview.

My response: *"What...?"*

"Nope," said one of them. "I've never, ever had to interview for a job. I just knew somebody or had the right contact, and I got the job."

This astounded me. It truly shows how much the world of business has changed.

In all the years I've been working, I have never been lucky enough to be given a job based entirely on who I knew. Sure, I was fortunate enough to have people try to *recruit* me, but I still had to go through the application and interview process. What this tells me is that millennials are very good at leveraging their networks. They activate the network, and the jobs come to them.

The traditional way of seeking job openings and interviewing for positions is on its way out. This is just further evidence of how dramatically different the professional world is today than it was for our parents and grandparents. The idea of finding a steady job and working for the same employer for twenty years is a thing of the past. I could *never* work at the same place for twenty years!

In my professional life I was moving on to the next thing every three years or so. I wanted to come in, work hard, fix what was broken, get it going, and then move along. I needed fresh challenges and that is exactly the mindset that millennials and Generation X share. They arrive, put in their contribution, and then they are on to the next thing. The idea that you need an employer, steady hours, and benefits is something I do not see with millennials. They know you can create your workspace, work remotely, and set your own hours—and they absolutely love that. They want that freedom.

This is a new attitude that is difficult for older generations to comprehend. In fact, I was talking to my sister recently. She is thirty-eight, works full-time, and needs to get a second job for a couple of hours a week. She's a single mom and still thinks traditionally. She had the mindset that she needed *hours*—that if you want to work, you need to find an opening somewhere, go for an interview, and get a job with an employer that fits in within your schedule.

I said, "You know, you don't have to do that anymore. Companies, contacts, and entrepreneurs all need virtual assistants or other work done remotely. It's a great way to reduce costs. You don't need an employer. All you need is a laptop and a cell phone."

While baby boomers are out looking for *jobs*, young professionals are looking for meaningful *work*. They're not afraid to cold-call. If they see something on social media, they're not afraid to just put their résumé in for consideration. Before a baby boomer even thinks of submitting a résumé, a millennial has already looked up the company on LinkedIn and is direct-messaging the decision-maker to say, "Hey, I see you need some help. We already have four different connections in common, so feel free to talk to any of them." They haven't even officially applied for the job, and they've already jumped the queue all the way to the reference call!

Baby Boomers will go along through the process passively, interview, wait to hear if they made the cut, ask about the benefits structure and the hours. Meanwhile, if a millennial gets to the point where they're a good fit for the organization, they're asking, "Do I have the flexibility to work from home? Do I have to go to an office setting? What is the reporting structure?"

The bottom line is, young professionals today have a *contractor* mindset versus an *employee* mindset.

Today's Millennial Working Woman

I noticed that millennial women tend to make decisions based on the economics and logistics of their situation. In the past, men and women assumed societal roles and professional opportunities based on a sense of duty or obligation. Millennials, on the other hand, tend to weigh the pros and cons of their life decisions and do what *makes sense.*

In fact, despite riding the proverbial waves of change, most millennials' homes are pretty traditional. I see a healthy mix of fathers doing more at home and sharing the workload. I also see an *increased* prevalence of millennials harkening back to more traditional roles, which I did not expect.

This might seem counterintuitive, but it's not that millennial women feel obligated to stay at home; it just doesn't always make sense for them to work. If, say, the cost of childcare means the family would end up almost breaking even if mom went to work, then they're going to do what makes the most financial sense. When I talk to millennial men, I ask, "Does your wife work *inside* the home, or *outside* the home?" And what I find is that if the female does not work outside the home, it isn't because of any sense of obligation or duty. Instead, the explanation is usually something like, "At the end of the day, when we run the numbers, it doesn't make sense."

In previous generations, there was also a greater concern around supporting the household, having a stable income, and being able to rely on a job. Millennials tend not to worry so much about those things. They're apt to do what they feel is best for them. Instead of saying, "I hate this job, but I must grin and bear it," they say, "I hate this job, so I'm going to leave. Something else will come along, or I will create my own opportunity."

This is a huge departure from the traditional way of thinking about a career. Years ago, the trajectory was: Work somewhere for a *minimum* of five years, get the experience, then move on to somewhere else. That five-year minimum was because you wanted it on your résumé. You did not want to look like you hopped around. Millennials do not think that way.

It is a changing world. It is still a precarious climb for a young woman to attain success in a leadership position in the business world, but its arguably more achievable now than it has ever been in history.

It's never been easier to jump the queue.

Standing on My Own Two Feet

When I think about my own experiences, I realize I have been jumping the queue my whole life. Much like the millennial woman of today, I never waited for opportunities. I never settled. I was always seeking more, always forging my own path to find an opportunity—writing my own rulebook to become a leader.

Like many people, I come from a divorced home. My father was an alcoholic, a drug addict, and suffered from manic depression. He was what people now call a functioning alcoholic. My parents were bright people. Both were the first in their families to graduate from college. My father was the only one out of his five brothers to go to college. He became a successful lawyer, and my mother was a schoolteacher and the first female accepted into the College of Engineering at the University of Florida. My parents both valued education highly. I think that was the original glue that held them together. My father was a well-known attorney, but by the time I was eight, he had gotten into drugs and alcohol. That lifestyle led him down a very slippery slope and inevitably, it created conflict at home. I was always walking on eggshells in our household, and when I was about ten years old, my parents went through a nasty divorce, complete with custody battles.

I ended up with my mom, but when I was fourteen, I decided I wanted to go live with my father. I never really got to know him growing up because he had been busy building his law practice, and I wanted the chance to know my father better. It was during that time that I learned the full scope of his sickness. In addition to drug and alcohol abuse, his manic depression caused unpredictable mood swings. Witnessing this firsthand led me to realize how bad things had become.

In the 1980s, you did not talk about mental illness. It was not understood or treated the way it is now. Culturally, and in that corporate world, it was not something that was accepted. My father had no one to help him, so I was thrust into the role of being the adult in the house prematurely. At fourteen, I was doing a lot of the household chores, laundry, cooking, shopping, and cleaning. I couldn't just be a kid. I couldn't act like a normal teenager. Not when I was dealing with a father who would drink and pass out at home.

The only upside was that he did quite well in his work, so I always assumed his finances were in order and my college education was safe. I was accepted to Boston University to study under Nobel Laureate and Holocaust survivor Elie Wiesel. When I proudly presented my letter of acceptance to my father, it never occurred to me that not attending might be an option. However, at the tune of $27,000 a year, I was told that although he was very proud of me for getting in, we just did not have the money.

"Anyways, why would you want to go so far away?" he said. "It is so damn cold there. A Florida school will give you just as good an education." He smiled sarcastically and added, "And you will be closer to me."

I was baffled, but it seemed like there was nothing I could do.

I decided to go as far north as I could, to a town I knew my father would never visit. He referred to it as "Tallahickie," even though it was his alma mater and he was among the first graduating class of their law school. Yes, Tallahassee was the perfect choice! I would get my bachelor's degree there, and eventually, if I went to grad school, I would go to Boston University as I'd hoped.

I'll never forget walking into Burt Reynolds Hall to see the financial aid officer for the fourth time during the Fall semester of my junior year in 1994. For my first two semesters of college, my parents had been able to afford my tuition and living expenses. But I soon learned the real reason I hadn't been able to go to Boston University. It seemed my father's finances weren't as secure as I had assumed.

For some reason, my dad failed to pay his income taxes for a few years. Consequently, his wages were now being garnished. He was on the precipice of filing for bankruptcy. The problem I now faced was that in order to qualify for financial aid was based on the *prior* year's tax returns, which meant that on paper, I was not a candidate for assistance.

As I sat in the waiting area, it was incomprehensible to me that there had been no plan to send me to college. I felt defeated and humiliated, and now, I would have to explain to the financial aid officer yet again why the daughter of a successful lawyer needed assistance in paying for her education.

"Michelle McQuillan," the officer called.

I walked over and sat at his desk, anticipating the bad news, while he reviewed the notes in my file. So far, I had been turned down for every type of grant and loan out there except for an unsubsidized Stafford loan—a loan that was not predicated on financial need and incurred interest at the time of the dispersal of funds. It was not preferred. However, if I was granted *anything* today, I would gladly accept it and move on. It would be in my name, and paying it off would be nobody's responsibility but my own.

"What is your major?" asked the financial aid officer.

"Humanities with a minor in Classical Civilization," I answered.

Almost immediately, I could sense his disappointment that I was not one of the thousand Business or Communications majors at the university. "What are you going to do with that?" he said with a confused look.

After two semesters as a Humanities major, I knew one thing: I was going to make a living traveling the world, as far away from home as possible.

I looked the financial aid officer in the eye and answered with confidence, "That's funny. I guess I've always thought—what *can't* I do with it?"

He stamped my paperwork and did not even look up as he said, "Well, you may want to rethink your course of study, as you may not be able to afford to pay back this loan with that major."

But I could not even respond to his comment because of the elation jolting through my body. The loan was approved! This meant I could continue my education. Although I would be in debt, I was staying. Little did I know that signing that paperwork was the first step toward independence from my father and the start of a new way of how I looked at the choices in my life.

When I returned to my dorm and opened the door, my roommate, who was also on financial assistance, said to me, "And are you now joining the rest of us who have to pay their own way?"

I replied, "Yes. Yes, I am."

From then on, I was running on my own steam and no one else's. I put myself through school, and I had to take a lot of loans to do it. I was getting straight As. I was tutoring athletes on the side, I was a note taker for students with learning disabilities, and I was doing whatever I could to earn extra money. When I came home during semester breaks, I would take jobs to earn money for the next semester so I could focus on my studies.

During my final year at Florida State, I was given the opportunity to study abroad in Florence, Italy. That experience made all those loans worth it. It was a time I will always treasure because it continued to build my confidence. As I traveled throughout Europe, I finally saw firsthand the art I had been studying for over two years.

I probably would have stayed in Italy, as I had a job offer to serve as the registrar at the Peggy Guggenheim Museum in Venice, but a mentor explained to me that if I stayed and pursued my graduate degree in Italy, it may not be equivalent if I returned to the United States. I did not want to do double the work, so I returned to Tallahassee for graduation. I had my sights set on returning to Italy one day to assume a curator role in the area of fifteenth-century Italian Renaissance.

Through these opportunities, I met new people, collected new experiences and was exposed to a degree of normalcy. I was able to see what the world could be. That was when I started to truly realize how *not* normal my household and family life had been while growing up.

***

I graduated from Florida State magna cum laude and took a job in Vero Beach, Florida. In 1997, after two years of working as a registrar at the Center for the Arts, I realized one thing:

I needed to get out of Vero Beach—or "Zero Beach," as the locals referred to it—and work on my master's degree.

I was determined to return to Italy. I just had to complete my master's degree and find a way to study in Paris to complete the initial research on an Italian fresco set in the loggia of the Louvre Museum.

For the next few months, I studied for the graduate entrance exam (GRE) and once again applied to schools. Boston University was at the top of my list, of course, and the University of South Florida was third, for financial reasons. But why would I not get into BU? At FSU I had straight A's, two years of work experience, and great letters of recommendation. However, this time around, I was not accepted. There was no slot available to apprentice with a professor in my area of study. In the end, and due to it being on my dime, I graciously accepted the offer from the small but opportunistically appealing Art History department at the University of South Florida. I was accepted at USF on a graduate assistantship, meaning they were going to pay 60 percent of my tuition.

Although I had great anxiety about moving home and being closer to my father, who still medicated his professional and personal pain with drugs and alcohol, I began to plan my exit from Vero Beach. It was the beginning of a period when I saw another, even darker side of my father.

All the experiences I gained in college had taught me a newfound sense of independence regarding what I did with my life, how I carried myself, and who I dated. Anything that threatened my father's patriarchal role—his authority over me—angered him tremendously. It was strange to me. I had lived on my own. I was an adult. I could not understand what made him think that he had the right to control what I did. Things had always been bad, but this was new—a manipulative, controlling side of him. I had always had a lot of anxiety as a kid as a result of my home life, and it was like my father was trying to turn me into that child again. But now, I knew how to deal with that, and my father didn't like it very much.

The best thing I did at that time—maybe the smartest thing I've done in my entire life—was to see a psychologist and psychiatrist. They gave me strategies to start honing in on how to set up healthy boundaries for dealing with an alcoholic parent with manic tendencies. We called it "adding tools to your toolbox."

The motivation wasn't so much about the anxiety I was experiencing; it was about acknowledging my own risk of falling into a similar patterns down the road, and learning how to circumvent that possibility. Thankfully, I stayed in therapy throughout the time I lived in Vero Beach. It made all the difference in how I re-entered my move back home and how I interfaced with my father and others throughout my life who had a similar nature.

The sad fact is that a lot of women who come from dysfunctional families, where verbal and physical abuse is present, end up in similar circumstances with their own husbands or significant others later in life. They end up leaving one dysfunctional life behind for another, and they blame their parents. I knew that if I ever were to get married or be with somebody, I didn't want that to happen to me. I wanted to learn the lesson, get over it, and figure out how to heal and move on.

A lot of the things I've gone through in my personal and professional life have come down to that attitude— learning the lesson, achieving what I'm supposed to get out of a situation, getting over it, and getting on with it. That's really what this book is about: cutting through the barriers. There came a point when I didn't want to wait on the opportunity for somebody to give me a job. I worked in the museum world, where jobs are few and far between. Most major cities have only a few museums, and there isn't a high turnover rate; people in museum jobs stay forever. So, part of what I had to learn was how to be creative in finding new job opportunities.

"Grave Robbers"

While I was planning my return to Tampa to work on my master's degree at USF, I discovered that the Florida International Museum in St. Petersburg was looking for a contract registrar to handle the shipping and installation of artifacts for its next exhibition, *Titanic: The Exhibition*. Although it was not an accredited museum but more of a traveling exhibition hall, I was intrigued by the prospect of a job, the pay, and working with artifacts from the *Titanic*.

Prior to moving to Vero Beach, I had worked on two exhibitions at the same museum, *Treasures of the Czars* and *Alexander the Great*. Thus, I was already familiar with the organization and their internal processes of exhibition production.

Besides being a great opportunity, accepting the job with the *Titanic* was a positive connection with my father. From a young age, I had shared his love of the sea. I was raised in Bradenton, Florida, and there was not much else to do but go to the beach or fish. My father had always made sure we lived on the water—on the ocean, on a canal, or by a lake—and we always took the boat out every chance we could to ride, ski, snorkel, or scuba dive. Vacations were spent in Key West where we would spearfish all day long and play in the hotel pool until dusk, then eat our day's catch and watch the sunset. My father rarely drank with us during these times because he needed to "be present."

The morning after I accepted the temporary position with the *Titanic* exhibition, I walked in to give my notice to the executive director of the Center for the Arts and let him know I was going to begin my master's degree and work on the *Titanic* exhibition, which was already receiving quite a bit of attention. He smiled, stood up from his desk, and pulled an article from a recent newspaper.

As he handed me the article, which discussed the impending exhibition, he looked at me and said, "I understand that you want to get your master's degree, and you did say you would only give us two years, but you're such a bright girl. Do you really want to work for a bunch of grave robbers?"

Looking back now, I know I did not fully realize the depth of his question, but his tone seemed familiar to me. It was a tone of voice that I would continue to be sensitive to throughout my life. It carried an undercurrent of belittlement or doubt, meant to encourage me to do what *he* felt was the right thing—much like that financial advisor at FSU years before. But the "right thing" for who?

Sometimes, you need to forge your own path to learn for yourself what the right thing is.

Of course, I was only twenty-three at the time and very naïve, but I did know this: This was a once-in-a-lifetime opportunity and one I did not want to miss. I proudly answered, "I do not think I'll be thought of as a 'grave robber.' In fact, I think just the opposite. I think there are many others who would want this chance, and they chose me. Thank you for your concern, but I am moving forward with this decision."

As I turned and walked away, I couldn't help but wonder, was he right? But it didn't matter. The next step in my academic career was waiting. Plus, what if I did such a good job for the company that they wanted to hire me full-time? What if I could even dive the wreck of the Titanic in a deep sea submersible one day?

What if?

Chapter 2

Develop Your Moral Compass

"Great people do things before they're ready."
—Amy Poehler

Getting the job at the Titanic exhibition meant that I would not have to take loans for grad school. I could pay for my school while *going* to school. What a novel idea.

It was the best of both worlds, but it would not be without its challenges. Every explorer needs a compass, and when you are jumping the queue and forging your own path, there is arguably nothing more important than a developing a moral compass.

In August of 1997, I began to focus in the evening on my graduate studies and worked during the day on the *Titanic* exhibition. The exhibition was organized by RMS Titanic Inc., who had the salvor-in-possession rights to the wreck. That meant they alone were permitted to gather artifacts from the wreck of the *RMS Titanic*, conserve, and exhibit them for public display.

For all practical purposes, the *Titanic* exhibition was a "canned exhibit," in the sense that it was pre-curated by a team of historians, then transported to various sites around the world. I worked alongside Steve Massler, the curator from a Memphis, Tennessee company called The Wonders International Cultural Series. I also worked with fine art shipping and installation coordinator Leroy Pettyjohn, also from Memphis. He worked with Mallory Alexander International Logistics. Both were familiar with the installation of the exhibition and also assisted in hiring local crews to help meet our November 15 deadline, when we were scheduled to open to the public.

We worked six days a week to prepare for the opening of the highly-anticipated exhibition at the Florida International Museum. The city of St. Petersburg had already enjoyed a surge of culture with the *Treasures of the Czars exhibition*, and the downtown area was transforming into a cultural hub as a result. It did not hurt that James Cameron's much-anticipated *Titanic* movie was about to hit theatres. Timing was truly on our side.

Each day was filled with excitement as we unpacked crates filled with treasures from the depths of the ocean. Some days, we staged the opening of crates for the media while other days, we would work diligently, behind closed doors, to ensure that each artifact was inspected, accounted for, and ultimately installed.

I learned so much during that time, and no job was too small. Many things had to be done on the fly, and flexibility was key. If it was building crates from scratch, we did it. If it meant using a walk-behind pallet jack to drop in exhibition cases and secure them to the ground to meet anti-theft precautions, we accomplished it. I developed a great relationship with Leroy, as our work ethic and intense nature seemed to go hand-in-hand.

During this time—and, in fact, over the course of the next two years—I did not let anyone at school know I was already working in the field. Partly, this was because working for a for-profit venture versus a "nonprofit museum" was frowned upon in elite museum circles. As my former boss had so eloquently put it, many within our field saw us as "grave robbers."

In my opinion, however, the practices were the same. The only difference was the size of the budget ... and pay! There was *no* budget. You did whatever you could to get the exhibition opened while maintaining the highest level of professionalism. Money was invested by the city, investors, colleges, and companies, and the expected return was high attendance and recognition. It was incongruent to the small budget of nonprofit museums and local publicity, but this was what made the effort and the risk so exciting.

41

I also learned a lot about the business aspects of such a venture as it related to shareholder value and hostile takeovers.

Above all, I would soon learn what *risk* truly meant.

***

Ultimately, *Titanic: The Exhibition* opened successfully and during its six-month run it topped out at 830,000 visitors.

This type of attendance was rarely seen by museums to date, with the exception of the blockbuster King Tut exhibition at the Metropolitan Museum of Art from 1976 to 1979, which drew in over eight million people in its three-year run. It felt great to have taken this chance and to be associated with such an exciting project.

I would have been searching for new employment immediately after the exhibition opened in November had I not been working with Leroy Pettyjohn or had a chance meeting with a man named G. Michael Harris. Instead, two days before the end of the installation, Leroy asked me over lunch if I wanted to come work for his company, Alexander International, when the exhibition was slated to close in May, to assist with the de-installation. I agreed and was ecstatic to have a job lined up. And so, after a grueling two months of installations of room-by-room recreations, I was soon learning how to secure exhibitions cases to the floor using two two-by-fours and a shotgun loaded with rubber bullets.

As the months passed, I continued to focus on school and, because I was paid so well, I was even able to take a few months off. In May, the team was reassembled, and we de-installed the exhibition. As we packed up the show, Leroy asked if I wanted to intern with him for the summer in Memphis. I would spend the majority of the summer setting up blockbuster traveling exhibitions. I had an internship requirement for my graduate program. Typically, this was spent at the USF Contemporary Art Museum, but, by hook and crook, the internship with Leroy was approved. He was also able to ensure it was a paid position, so it was a win-win for everyone.

What I didn't anticipate during this time was meeting the love of my life, Eric, in March of 1998. My goal had always been to come home from studying abroad in Italy for two years, gain work experience, achieve my master's degree, then head back to Italy. I never thought for a minute that I would be so lucky in love while simultaneously excelling in my studies and my professional career.

Eric traveled quite a bit and was supportive of my situation. It was hard, but we agreed I needed to move to Memphis for the summer and gain the experience working for a shipping company. His largest client, Federal Express, was based in Memphis, and we had high hopes of making it work. I packed up my car in the summer of 1998 with no idea what was in store for me.

On the Road

I arrived in Memphis and was thrown immediately into a freight shipping, custom work, and contract exhibition installation.

Over the next six weeks, I traveled to Jackson, Mississippi to work on the French exhibition *Splendors of Versailles*, then on to Delaware to install the Russian exhibition *Nicholas and Alexandra*, and then on to Boston to install the *Titanic* exhibition from St. Petersburg. It was an incredibly interesting summer that I spent working with curators from all over the world. I had access to things most people would never have access to and handled everything from precious Fabergé eggs to priceless artifacts from the Palace of Versailles.

I learned what I liked best, which was the food—fried peach pies in the South, beer cheese soup in the North, and fried clams in the Northeast. I coordinated the transportation and customs paperwork with gritty truck drivers who lived out of their trucks, and I seemed to excel at negotiating and getting things done with various entities such as the unions, customs staff, and drivers.

I also learned what I did not like: arguing for over five hours with the Fish and Wildlife Service a plume feather that was to be strewn over the bed of King Louis for an exhibition. I mean, were we really going to hold up an entire shipment over a single rare feather? Yes. Yes, we were.

Sleep deprivation was also not my favorite. Having to be up for forty-eight to seventy-two hours straight to meet airline freights was never fun, but there were some memorable moments in which a rookie shipping coordinator could find humor—like spending the coldest night on record in Atlanta International Airport. Standing there, freezing, all I wanted to do was make sure our shipment was cleared. I boarded the double-decker airplane with four other shipment coordinators who were there to make sure their shipments made it safely. I could smell this strange stench, almost like I was in a circus tent.

Soon, I realized I could hear the chattering of monkeys, and when I asked what it was, one of the other shipping agents said, "They're monkeys infected with AIDS being shipped to Emory University for testing. They are on the level below." I thought to myself, *why would they have artifacts on this flight?* Later, I learned it was the most cost-efficient way to ship the cargo.

I was told not to go anywhere near the monkeys. No worries there.

I learned that I liked the travel, and it encouraged and reaffirmed for me that moving forward with my graduate work was worth taking seriously, as it meant working with curators from around the world. However, I also realized that freight shipping was not for me. The personal cost can be too great on loved ones. I witnessed the other side of strained marriages, affairs that would culminate after only for a few weeks in a contained, secure environment. It was a hard lesson to observe.

The best memory I had during that time that was when our team had to meet the first shipment of artifacts from Russia's Hermitage Museum. Our task was to arrange the transport of, among other things, the wedding coronation carriage of Czar Nicholas II and his wife Alexandra. The extravagant carriage is priceless—encrusted in 14-karat gold. Our job was to arrange its transportation and escort from New York City to Delaware, which involved coordinating four tractor-trailers, police escorts, drivers, permits, tolls, and delivery across three state lines.

I had already been up for forty-eight hours straight when we arrived to Jamaica, New York, but I was able to get about four hours of sleep before we met the shipment at La Guardia at 3:00 p.m. There was quite a bit of media attention. The bodies of Nicholas II and his family were being moved to a new resting place in Russia on the same day. (Their former burial site had been an unmarked grave not far from where the family had been assassinated.) With this in mind, the fear factor of logistics going haywire in the United States was high.

So, there I was, in the back of a cop car as part of our entourage. At first, I thought I would catch some shut-eye, but this was to no avail. It was five o'clock in the evening, meaning rush-hour traffic in New York City, and our entourage was stopping traffic.

The first rule of this sort of transport operation is not breaking up the entourage. This is all the more important *and* all the more difficult when your entourage consists of four tractor-trailers escorting priceless artwork and the aforementioned priceless coronation carriage. We had three patrol car escorts: one in front, one in back, and one that drove alongside to ensure that the public would not try to cut into the entourage line. In addition, they would speed ahead and clear the tolls for us. Once we reached the next state line, another set of patrol car escorts came into play. You could hear the helicopters above us, and we were holding up any cars attempting to get on the highway entrance ramps.

The excitement alone would have been enough to keep me awake, but there was another reason I couldn't sleep. I had to use the restroom. I asked our driver if we could pull off at the next rest stop. "Sure," he said. Then, to my surprise, he radioed the other patrol cars and tractor-trailers to announce that we *all* had to get off at the next rest area, just so I could relieve myself.

As we exited and entered the first rest area, I was so embarrassed to get out of the car, but this feeling quickly faded as I realized that it paled in comparison to the faces of the teenagers, who were just getting off work at that rest stop, at sight of our fleet and the number of cops rolling in. They didn't know if they were busted for something or what was happening.

Our patrol officer stepped up and asked if the restrooms were open or closed.

"Closed," said the frail-voiced youth.

The officer replied, "Then I need you to open them, as this young lady needs to use the lavatory."

What was the kid going to do—not open the door? With a police officer ordering him to, and three patrol cars parked in front of the building?

Back into the car, as we were headed toward the New Jersey state line, I could not help but think how cool that was, even if I was just a hired hand. Between the bypassing of the tolls and the clearing of traffic, I've never gotten to Delaware so fast.

An Offer of a Lifetime

After Delaware, I was flown to Boston to install the *Titanic* Exhibition at Pier Six. I was only supposed to be there for one week but ended up staying for four, partly because of the unions and partly due to the challenge of having to modify an exhibit for a tent rather than an exhibition hall.

Leroy did not accompany me this time. Instead, I worked alongside the president and the CEO of RMS Titanic Inc., George Tulloch, and Stephan Pennec, whose company LP3 had conserved most of the artifacts that had been extracted from the ocean floor. The conditions were not secure. There were continued stops and starts, working in the tent was cramped, and a long day of work ended by returning to a drab, uncomfortable hotel room. Leroy later apologized to me for having to stay in Boston so long under those work conditions. He truly did not realize how difficult it had been for everyone.

The man I worked alongside every day, George Tulloch, was leading RMS Tianic, Inc. at the time. George already trusted me and had taken a liking to me. He was always kind to me and was very passionate about the *Titanic*. I could never have predicted that this project would be the last time I would ever work with him. Nor could I have predicted what would eventually happen to him—personally or professionally. As it would turn out, Mike Harris would later complete a successful hostile takeover from George in the middle of the night and move the company's offices from Battery Park, New York to Clearwater, Florida. I had met Mike several times because he had served on the board of directors of RMS Titanic, Inc. Eventually I would go on to work for him and take the adventure of a lifetime.

Writing the Book

By this time, I had curated every type of *Titanic* exhibit you can think of, from the Science Center in Baltimore to Vegas, but Orlando was different because … well, because it was Orlando. It had to be *entertainment*.

Throughout this project, I felt like I had to make a lot of compromises for the sake of the entertainment value. For example, for an exhibit showcasing artifacts from the ship's dining hall, we had plates from first class, second class, and third class. The decision was made to pipe in cinnamon smells in order to provide an ambiance of being in the *Titanic* dining hall. I had to be the one to say, "That's awesome, but we have to fix the cases, because we can't expose the artifacts to artificial odors and chemicals."

We had paper artifacts in the exhibit, and the higher-ups wanted certain lighting in the room. I had to speak up and explain, "I understand, but these items are very sensitive. You have to maintain the proper light level."

Some of it was actually funny. At one point, Mike Harris was looking at the artifact cases and asked me, "Why are the exhibit cases so high?

"Well," I explained, "they have to be a certain height in case somebody's in a wheelchair."

One day in Orlando, Mike kneeled down in front of one of the cases.

I looked down at him and said, "What are you doing?"

"I'm seven years old," he said. "I can't see the case."

I just looked at him. It had never even occurred to me. I was used to the more elitist, educated environment. But, again, this was Orlando. The traffic in Orlando is not the same as Vegas or New York City.

Mike wanted to make this exhibit accessible to families and fun for children, which was part of the reason it was decided there would be a room of the exhibit where we dropped the temperature down to the same temperature as the night the ship sank. We were going to have an ice wall—an actual, artificial iceberg—and kids would be able to put their hands on it.

Moisture is the enemy when it comes to artifact preservation; the last thing you want near a display is *water*. And yet we had a chunk of real ice in an artificially cooled room, right there as part of the exhibit. In front of it was a case containing a deck chair salvaged from the wreck of the *Titanic*.

I had issues with this. What if something malfunctioned? I kept reminding Mike what would happen to that deck chair, and everything else in that room, if there was ever a power outage and our iceberg melted. He would get so frustrated. We had to compromise a lot.

I had never been in this type of environment. You would never see an iceberg made of real ice in a museum. That just would not happen. You would never have smells pumped in to set the atmosphere. But that was what we were doing. It was the entertainment side, not art—history made accessible to a different clientele. The whole process was a real struggle for me. I had been trained that this was simply not how you did things. The challenge was to protect the integrity of what we were doing while also meeting Mike halfway so we could draw in 800,000 people, make money, and have the highest-rated show. It was difficult, fun, and there were a lot of risks involved.

I remember once, while trying to meet Mike halfway on something yet again, a problem came up that had me stumped. I told Mike, "I don't know how we're going to do this."

I'll never forget what Mike said next.

"You know, Michelle, sometimes there's a book, and sometimes you write the book."

Mike used to say that all the time. As much as I disliked it, he was right. I had to come to terms with the idea that, sure, there are set processes and procedures, but sometimes you have to create those procedures yourself.

The idea of "writing the book" speaks to me. To this day, in my consulting work, not every client is cookie cutter. Not every business or organization is the same. This is yet another big difference between millennials and other generations.

A lot of millennials are writing the book. They are living in a time unlike any other, and they are figuring things out as they go. They are at the forefront of a major shift away from the old way of doing things, toward a new, more entrepreneurial spirit.

Mike Harris was an entrepreneur. He was a risk-taker. He was an investor. Everything was about shareholder value, and my job was to create that value. A lot of people I trained with in the finer museum profession were not happy that I had gone to the "blockbuster" exhibition side. But I always thought that if you really believe education should be accessible to everybody—and I do—then what's the problem? I felt good about doing these large blockbuster shows, because this population would never have walked into a fine arts museum.

Whether we were doing the *Titanic*, or *Treasures of the Czars*, or *Empires and Mystery*, or *Alexander the Great*, or the *Bodies* exhibit, the things we brought in allowed people to learn about history, art, and science while also being entertained. I was all for it. It made it different. It made it exciting. And it hadn't been done. We were "writing the book."

Setting Healthy Boundaries

It was around this time that I started to learn a key skill a professional woman must develop —how to create healthy boundaries.

When my father, for example, would ask me to join him for dinner, I would say, "Sure. I'd love to have dinner with you. But you can't drink." Or I'd tell him, "Sounds great, I'll meet you there," and I would be sure to take my own car.

He would say, "Why don't you want me to pick you up?"

I would come up with an excuse. The real reason was that I didn't want to ride in a car while my father was high. When you're a kid, you can't make that decision. You're stuck in the car with your parents, whether you like it or not. They are in total control, and you can't leave. You can't have boundaries.

One night, I drew my line in the sand. We were having dinner and hadn't even ordered our food yet, but he was already knocking back the drinks. I looked at him and said, "Thanks so much for dinner, but I'm going to excuse myself now."

The look on his face was pure shock. "You're leaving?" he said.

"Yes," I said. I had seen this play out far too many times. He would drink too much and be belligerent while I graciously made excuses to the wait staff for his rude behavior. I could already taste the disappointment in my mouth. I took a cab home. It was the first of three times, in particular, where I said, "This is not normal. This is not right."

Unfortunately, things went downhill from there. One of the worst incidents was when he wanted to visit our exhibit in

Orlando. I booked him a hotel room at the Peabody Hotel and said, "I'm going to ask you one favor. Please don't drink." I was nervous but happy that he would be there on opening night to see what I had accomplished.

My sister and I have always had a code when it comes to our parents, as a means of warning one another. Things like, "They're acting weird," or, "Stay away from Dad today." In this case, my sister contacted me and gave it to me straight: "He drank an eight-pack on the way over, Michelle."

That night at the exhibit, Eric was in the bathroom, and my father came in, stumbling around with a bottle of beer in his hand. Eric and I were dating at the time, so he knew my dad had problems. He said, "You know, Charlie, just put the beer down. Michelle asked you not to drink."

My father was a mean drunk. He looked at Eric, then took the bottle and just slammed it against the counter.

That was the first time Eric really understood. Up until that point, I would tell him stories, and he would say, "Yeah, but he is your father...." But that night, Eric told me, "I've never encountered a drunk like that. I've never seen anything like that."

"*Now* do you get it?" I said. "Now do you understand how bad this is?"

***

Things became even nastier and uglier after that. I'll spare the details, but suffice it to say, there was a lot of harassing and hostile behavior. I finally decided enough was enough, and it was time to get a restraining order against my father.

Of course, that is easier said than done in a town where every attorney and every judge knows your father—and probably was partying with him at the time. I walked into a well-known family law attorney's office in South Tampa and shared my story with him. I had many of my father's threats on tape. The attorney looked at me and said, "Michelle, you are a smart girl. You can pay me $1,000 and I can file the restraining order, or you could save yourself the money and file it yourself."

He was right, I could. I worked in my father's law office for years. All it would take was time and perseverance. It was the first time I realized what my mother must have gone through in divorcing my father. The roadblocks, the lack of support, and the fact he knew everyone in town made it difficult. Regardless, I was not going to be deterred.

I did all the paperwork myself, and everywhere I went, people would recognize my last name. "Is this your father? You sure you want to do this to your father?" It was amazing how much grief I was given about filing a restraining order against my father. Every time somebody would ask me if I was sure I wanted to go through with it, I'd have to relive the experience and tell them, "Oh, I'm sure. I'm *positive*. My mom was not able to accomplish this when we were little, but it stops here. I don't want this in my life."

I had to go in front of a judge who knew my father well, and my father was there in the courtroom with a friend to represent him. I had recordings of messages where Father had threatened to kill me.

The judge said, "Michelle, what do you want?"

I said, "I just want him to stay away from me. Please grant the restraining order."

I remember they paused because my father's attorney said, "We've not heard any of these tapes."

The judge allowed him to play the tapes, in my presence in the hallway. I watched my father's attorney play the tape and fumble with the recorder as if he did not know how to use it, and then erased a portion of the tape. It didn't matter. I had four hours of his rants taped. My father's attorney and family friend looked at me and said, "Are you sure you want to do this and play this publicly? Your father will be crushed." I looked at him and nodded yes.

Fortunately, it didn't matter that a portion of the tape was gone. I looked forward and never made eye contact with my father while his drunken voice played so all in the courtroom could hear his tirade. I was granted the restraining order for one year. It was the most peaceful year of my 20s.

A lot happened in that year, including something I never could have predicted. One day, Mike Harris told me, "We're going on an expedition to the *Titanic* in 2000, and we need somebody onboard the research vessel to curate the artifacts we bring up. Do you want to come?"

I graduated with magna cum laude with my master's degree on May 11, 2000, was married on May 13 (with an undercover cop at my wedding and my mother by my side walking me down the aisle), and was out at sea by July 7 on an expedition that would lead to me diving to the wreck of the *Titanic* in a deep-sea submersible. Talk about jumping the queue.

The restraining order gave me the space I needed to not have that type of drama in my life anymore and time to understand what I value. If I could stand up to my father, I knew I could stand up to anyone.

Exercise: Develop Your Personal Values

1. Make a list of the things you value.
2. How are you implementing them in your life?
3. Rate the list in order of importance and begin to incorporate them into your life.

This exercise always helps me to take responsibility for my life and prioritize my choices.

Chapter 3

Diving the Titanic

"I look to the sea
Reflections in the waves spark my memory
Some happy, some sad
I think of childhood friends and the dreams we had
We live happily forever, so the story goes
But somehow we missed out on that pot of gold
But we'll try, best that we can
To carry on."

—STYX, "COME SAIL AWAY"

I am twenty-seven and freshly married, and four weeks later I am on my way to the North Atlantic on my own, headed for the *Titanic*.

As part of the preparations for the journey, I make out a will, which feels strange for someone my age. Although I love my husband, I don't want to sign over *everything*. Not that we have much; I just don't even know him that well! It is surreal to think that this is supposed to be our first year of marriage.

I had hesitated about going on the expedition in the first place. But I thought, *if there is a chance to even be part of this, I have to be there. And if there's a chance to dive, I want to do it. I want to be a part of that.*

So, off I go to the middle of the North Atlantic for eight weeks.

We leave out of Norfolk, Virginia on a ship we soon discover is not equipped for the raging seas of the North Atlantic. We have to fire the company in the middle of the ocean and switch to a more suitable vessel: the *Akademik Keldysh*, the largest oceanographic research vessel in the world. It is the same ship featured during the present-day scenes in the movie *Titanic*.

The wreck of the *Titanic* is located in the Flemish Cap, east of Newfoundland and Labrador. You can only be at sea in that region for about eight weeks out of the year because of the weather patterns, the rough seas, and hurricane season. But eight weeks in the North Atlantic is a long time to be at sea. And it's not for everybody.

We're in the middle of nowhere. You can't see land and there is almost zero contact with the outside world. One might get a few minutes with a satellite phone once in a while or maybe an email.

A lot of people start to freak out. I watch men look out the vessel's portholes, unable to see land, and have episodes—grown men who could not deal with cabin fever. They have never been away that long. We have to ship people back home. Not everybody can do it. I don't know if I can do it, either. There's no way to know except to keep on trying.

***

The Royal Mail Ship *Titanic* went down in the icy waters of the North Atlantic on April 15, 1912. Of the roughly 2,200 people who were aboard the ship, over 1,500 of them died that day. Since then, fewer people have visited the *Titanic* than have been to space. One of our goals for our 2000 expedition was to see the ship and to use submersibles to recover new artifacts for the RMS Titanic Inc. traveling exhibition. As holder of the salvor-in-possession rights to the *Titanic*, we were the only company allowed to salvage the wreck.

There are exceptionally rough seas in the Flemish Cap. (If you've ever seen the movie *The Perfect Storm*, that's where the events took place.) The best time to go is between the beginning of July till about the end of August, which is the calmest time of the year. We were moved off-site twice for hurricanes.

Just getting to the location of the wreck was an adventure in itself. My biggest fear was that I would get seasick. They had something called the scopolamine patch, which was an adhesive patch meant to help with motion sickness, but still, many people simply can't handle it.

And then there were the dives. It's about two-and-a-half miles to the ocean floor where the *Titanic* lies. If you tried to reach that depth in a typical Navy sub, the pressure would crush the hull, and everything inside would implode. There are only six submarines in the world that can reach those depths. Two are in America at Woods Hole National Geographic Institute in New England, where Bob Ballard – who discovered the Titanic – worked. Two are in France, at the French oceanographic institute IFREMER. And two are with the *Akademik Keldysh*. These are known as the *Mir-1* and *Mir-2* submersibles.

Each *Mir* submersible cost over $25 million to build. They are three-person subs built from titanium and high-grade rolled steel made to withstand 6,000 pounds of pressure per square inch. They weigh around eighteen tons apiece. The viewing ports have to be tiny. Any larger and the submersible would implode under the enormous pressure of the sea. Any larger and the submersible would implode under the enormous pressure. Some people can't go in the subs. There are no lavatories, and if you're claustrophobic, forget about it.

I didn't know if I'd ever see the inside of one of those subs. My job was to be a curator of the artifacts that were brought up, meaning I would get to handle items that had not been above water for over a hundred years, before they ever went public. I would be working in the lab onboard the ship. It was never a sure thing that *I* would get to dive down in a sub and actually see the ship myself, but, of course, the possibility was always in the back of my mind.

There I was, with only one other woman and all these men, working a schedule of forty-eight hours straight, followed by one day off, and followed by forty more hours straight. Our team worked around the clock to process the artifacts being brought up from the dives, seven days a week, and it was great. It was exhausting, but great. We ran on pure adrenaline. It was such a rush to see what came out of the subs. It was so humbling working with things like suitcases and seeing hundred-year-old clothes packed for destinations that were never reached.

The spotlight on what we were doing was incredible. We had constant media coming in and out, *USA Today*, *National Geographic*. It wasn't the *Tampa Bay Times* anymore—it was *The Today Show*.

It was the most focused I have ever been in my life. There were zero distractions—nothing to do but think about your work. You're not grocery shopping. You're not driving anywhere on a daily commute. We had a crew that did our laundry. All you had to do was get up in the morning, do your job for sixteen hours, sleep, and do it all over again the next day.

My First Dive

I was lucky enough to dive to the *Titanic* twice. Some people on the vessel had gotten sick during the eight weeks at sea, so I was asked to take another person's place.

On the morning of my first dive, I was ready at 6:00 a.m. on August 4, 2000, and the ship's crane released our sub into the waters by 8:00 a.m. I was diving with Ralph White who holds the record for participating in the most expeditions to the Titanic wreck site (13) and the American with the most dives (35). Ralph was there in 1987 when the wreck was located and contributed his documentarian skills over the years. He is also a noted cinematographer for National Geographic. I was truly honored to be in his presence and in awe of his explorations, nuggets of knowledge and wry sense of humor. We descended beneath the ocean, knowing that we wouldn't be above water again for thirteen hours.

The compartment crew in a *Mir* submersible is seven feet in diameter and accommodates three people—a pilot, a copilot, and an observer—who each have a one-foot-thick plastic porthole between themselves and the depths. Picture yourself inside a tiny submarine, slowly sinking below the surface of the ocean. Three of you are crammed into a space as big as a queen-sized bed. You can barely move, there are no bathrooms, and each dive could last between twelve to fourteen hours. I remember being told that each hour in the sub cost the company nearly $1,500. But compare that to what a private tourist dive pays, which, if I recall, costs in the neighborhood of $3,000 an hour.

The sub moves at a very slow pace. It takes around two and a half hours to reach the ocean floor—12,500 feet down. It takes at least another two and a half hours to come back up, closer to three hours if you come up heavy with artifacts in the baskets, collected with the sub's electronic arms.

Clearly, a twelve- to fourteen-hour trip means that going to the bathroom could become a big deal. I even bought Depends and wore them just in case. In the end, the *man-bottle* is the only lavatory—and a reason why many women do not dive the wreck. It worries you at first, but then you just get over it. When you gotta go, you gotta go.

It's very hot when you first go down, but by the time you get to the bottom, it's freezing, so you start the journey sweltering and dressed in several layers of clothing. Time is of the essence. If you run out of oxygen, you will suffocate. Plus, you're constantly exhaling carbon dioxide, so there are "scrubbers" that scrub the CO_2 out of the atmosphere of the sub to prevent CO_2 poisoning.

In addition to general discomfort, claustrophobia, and oxygen supply, there are other health risks. In such a highly oxygen-rich environment, any sort of fire or spark would rage out of control within seconds—total combustion. There is also the possibility of freezing to death or, of course, drowning if anything goes wrong. Plus, with 6,500 pounds of pressure per square inch bearing down on you, if something were to pierce the titanium hull, you would implode in half a second. Your brain wouldn't even register what had happened.

To give you some idea of the risks involved, during our expedition we learned that a Russian sub had experienced a malfunction and had gone down in the North Atlantic not far from us. There were three men trapped inside. We were diving on that day and were asked at one point if we could move off-site, presumably to stand by for a rescue attempt. But any sort of rescue would have been impossible. We were too far away to do anything, and even if we had been closer, what could we have done? It's two and a half miles down, with the weight of the entire ocean bearing down on you. You can't exactly open the door and let them in like a couple of hitchhikers. Hauling their sub up wasn't possible, either. There was no practical way to latch on, and even if there had been, they would have run out of oxygen long before we arrived—let alone by the time a slow-moving sub managed to pull their heavy vessel all the way up from the ocean floor. The three gentlemen died. It was inevitable. It was an international tragedy and a huge news story in the States. We received a lot of negative press for that. In fact, the story was still in the news when we returned home.

The descent to the ocean floor is like a free fall. The idea is to conserve all the available battery power. With every passing meter, pressure increases and sunlight diminishes. You're looking at nothing but water for ten hours straight, and that view gradually gets darker and darker. At 300 meters, it is already very dark, and the temperature of the water drops quickly. The scene transitions from a beautiful undersea world to pitch black. The pressure can reach up to 400 times that of the surface. The water temperature drops to 34°F outside the sub—just above freezing—and temperatures inside the sub drop from 95°F to 65°F. Suddenly, you are thankful for those layers of clothing.

There is very little sea life at these depths. There are the aptly named rattail fish—small colorless fish with tails like rats that spend their entire lives without ever seeing the sun. And there are some starfish. That's it.

When you finally land on the ocean floor, you immediately boot on the boomers (the lights) and the propellers to troll the bottom of the ocean, searching for artifacts through tiny portholes about ten inches in diameter. Artifacts are recovered using the manipulators of the submersible and special tools such as a modified suction apparatus for recovering delicate items, placing them in padded recovery baskets on the underside of the sub. If you see something while trolling, you really need to slow down because if you go over it and have to back up, it kicks up all the sand, which takes forever to clear.

For legal reasons, we were not allowed to touch the actual ship or take anything from within it. We were limited to gathering items from around the ship. Initially, the restriction was to be respectful of the fact that there were bodies entombed within the ship. There aren't any skeletal remains, though. People always ask that. There are no longer any human remains. But these days, you still would never enter the ship for safety reasons. It's covered in "rusticles," icicle-like formations made out of rust. The ship is going to start to fall apart and disintegrate soon.

The court of Norfolk Virginia also had a clause that no entity could land on the *Titanic* or take anything from the actual ship. Thus, there were limits on what could be respectfully removed from the wreck. We could only gather items that had spilled out onto the ocean floor. The ship split into two when it sank. There's the bow, the stern, and an area in the middle we call "Hell's Kitchen," where a large variety of artifacts can be found, having spilled out of the ship. My job was to catalog the items we picked up and write down the x and y coordinates of their provenance for the records.

I didn't see the actual ship during the first dive, which was disappointing. We were required to work a certain area in Hell's Kitchen, and we weren't close enough to see the actual ship. That was the part of the grid that we were assigned to work. It was definitely a letdown to be so close to the ship and not see it, but I was thrilled to be there nonetheless.

The most difficult thing was to see all the shoes. When you realize that the shoes slipped off the feet of people who were drowning, most of whom didn't survive—it gives you an eerie feeling. I was not prepared for that.

We brought up some really interesting artifacts, including a second-class crystal carafe and a dinner plate. It was a truly amazing experience.

My second dive, however, was a completely different story.

My Second Dive

One night, Mike asked me to come see him. I was told that they needed me to do the dive scheduled for the following day because the sickness was working its way through the ship and I was one of the few on board who wasn't sick.

"Everybody's ill," he said. "Can you do it?"

I said, "Absolutely." I didn't tell my family I was going to dive that second time. The first time had been stressful enough for them.

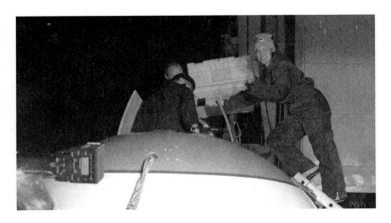

Just as we had on my first dive, we woke early on August 9, 2000, boarded the submersible, and descended into free fall. When we landed on the bottom of the ocean and turned on the lights, we saw some wreckage, but nothing registered on the sonar. Our pilot turned the sub to get a better view to figure out what we were seeing outside—tried to turn, anyway.

He couldn't turn.

It was a strange moment, to realize we couldn't turn left. *Is it a malfunction?* I wondered, which is not the sort of thing you want to be wondering 12,500 feet down at the bottom of the ocean.

All of a sudden, we heard a clicking sound. It echoed through the inside of the sub, and suddenly, I realized what it was. Scraping. The outside of the sub was scraping against something.

I don't think I said anything, but I was thinking, *stop whatever you're doing!* If something pierces the hull at those depths, we're not talking about a leak. We're talking about implosion. You're dead in half a second. I could not see anything out my porthole, and nothing was visible on the cameras. It was all just sand, water, and blackness.

"We obviously can't go to the left," said the pilot. "I'm going to try to steer us and put the propellers on, and we're going to go right."

As we turned, we felt something scratching the bottom, directly underneath our bodies. As our sub scraped against the unknown objects, two and a half miles beneath the ocean, with the entire weight of the sea bearing down on us, I thought, *Well, this is it.*

The pilot finally dislodged the sub from this unknown object, and we turned around. At first, we didn't know what we were looking at, we just saw red. Not sand. Just the color red, right in front of our faces.

"What is all that red?" we were asking one another.

Gradually, it dawned on us. It was rust. What we were looking at was the enormous, rust-coated hull of an *Olympic*-class ocean liner—one that had sunk to the bottom of the North Atlantic almost one hundred years prior.

"It's the ship," the pilot said. "It's *Titanic*.... It's the *Titanic*."

***

I'll never forget the feeling as we turned and realized the ship was *right there*. The thing we'd been scraping up against was the side of the *Titanic*.

Nothing can prepare you for the sheer size of the ship, let alone the realization of what you're looking at. I started to cry, my breath was taken away. It was surreal—the magnitude of where I was. It was incredible to think we had just *bumped into* the *Titanic*. We weren't even supposed to be that close, by law, but we hadn't realized where we were. We had dropped down almost on top of it. It wasn't reading on the radar because we were that close. We easily could have died. I just remember thinking, *I cannot believe what just happened*. But if I was going to die, where else would I want to be?

The pilot backed us away from the ship. We could see all the window panes that had been crushed when it sank. I was in awe. You cannot put it into words.

I had always pictured the *Titanic* the way it was in photos. Lying on the bottom of the sea, it obviously was not the majestic ship it had been in 1912. It was shattered and rusted, its glory days long gone. By the same token, I had an incredible sense of what had happened here. On my first dive, I really hadn't felt anything like that. Now, I realized that I was here, on the actual site where this disaster happened. I had been curating *Titanic* exhibits for years, but not until this moment did I understand the true scope of the tragedy—the enormity of this ship, and all these people who never made it to New York. It was really humbling. And really sad.

You cannot truly appreciate the size of the *Titanic* until you see it with your own eyes. We continued to troll around, and we saw the back of the propeller. It was giant. Just massive. It gave you an incredible sense of how huge the ship was. It was 175 feet high and 882 feet long—almost three football fields from end to end. How else can you say it? It was *huge*.

I was completely overwhelmed. I started tearing up when I thought about the enormity of the opportunity I had been given. Not many women had ever gotten here. I was one of twelve women in history to dive the wreck of the *Titanic* and the youngest female. I was only twenty-seven, yet they thought enough of me to bring me. I couldn't believe that three years before, when I had first started to work for this company, I had said, "Wouldn't it be amazing if I got to dive?"

And I did, I thought. *Here I am. I am actually doing this.*

And as we trolled along beside the ship, I remember thinking, *I would get out right now*. It sounds crazy, but in that moment, it felt like it would have been worth it—to open the hatch and get out, just to touch the ship, even if it meant dying at the bottom of the sea. I can't describe it any other way. I just wanted to get out of that sub. It was almost frustrating. I just didn't feel close enough, which was bizarre because I was closer than most humans will ever get. I wanted to get out and pick things up.

Later, I would read in the book *Titanic Adventure* by Jennifer Carter, the first woman to dive the *Titanic*, that she had a similar feeling:

> "[…] Nothing will ever match the moment when
> I went down to the ocean's depths and saw the

> *magnificent ruins of that great ocean liner, flooded by artificial light, as real to me as if it had been raised and lying on the surface. So real, that it was impossible to fathom the danger of being 12,500 feet below the sea. So real, that I had the impulse to open the door of the* Nautile *and swim out to greet it, swim inside its mysterious openings, up the grand stairs, into its ghost-like state rooms. How I wish I could survive in that 6,000 pounds per square inch pressure, so I could explore the wreck safely and forge an even more intimate bond with the ship."*

It was so quiet. It was so peaceful. When I die, I hope to have my ashes sprinkled over the wreck. I remember looking up at the side of this ship and thinking, *Life is good. I did it. I have accomplished everything I wanted. If it all ended today, it would be totally fine. This would be worth dying for.*

***

Of course, we had to get back to the business of doing what we came to do. We started picking up artifacts—first-class plates, tiles, lamps, a wok, and some interesting things like binoculars and thermometers. We had never gotten thermometers before.

Before I knew it, the pilot was saying, "Okay, we need to move on," and it was time to ascend. I couldn't believe it. The time went by so unbelievably fast. I wished I could stay just a little longer. Why couldn't somebody drop down extra oxygen, like when planes get refueled in mid-flight? Can't anybody do that?

To make matters worse, there was a hurricane upon us. They radioed to warn us ahead of time that when we surfaced, the seas were going to be really rough. I was worried our artifacts were going to break. *After all we've been through, we're going to lose everything.* Everything had looked so perfectly pristine down there. It was a nightmare to think we could bring it up, and it could all just break.

It was such a rude awakening to leave behind those silent, serene depths and come up in the middle of raging seas. I remember that night, after I had dinner, I was sitting with my copilot and friend Alfred Garr. We looked at each other and realized that no one would ever really understand what we had just done or experienced.

***

When all was said and done, our expedition recovered about 6,000 artifacts, and I processed every one of them in the ship's lab.

We always picked up bags if we had the chance, because you never knew what was in the bag. As you unpacked them, the contents often told the story. What was really wild was that you could sometimes even identify the owner. As we unloaded the sub's baskets after one of the dives, I kept smelling something and wondering what the smell was. Later, in the lab, I discovered a small bag containing shards of glass and small glass tubes. They were vials of oils. We were able to trace the oils back to the person who had been traveling with them. His name was Adolphe Saalfeld. Saalfeld, a first-class passenger and survivor, had been traveling from Paris to Macy's in New York to sell these oil concentrates for production as perfumes. You could still read the writing on the labels of his company and what type of oil it was.

The aromatic oils had been perfectly preserved in the vials and were just as strong as they had been eighty-nine years before. For several days in our lab, the smells of rose, lavender, and other scents became overwhelming. Later, visitors to our exhibition were able to "smell the *Titanic*" a hundred years later. *USA Today* loved that story. It was probably the biggest find of our expedition.

Back to Reality

At this point I had been working in museums for almost ten years. I had created so many of the exhibits memorializing the *Titanic*, but until the 2000 expedition, it had just been a job. After having seen the wreck with my own eyes, the level of responsibility changed. Now, it was something bigger. I felt a huge sense of duty to make sure that everything was being done tastefully. We were preserving something that future generations—my children—were going to get to see. Things that had been found on the bottom of the ocean floor, recovered so that anyone could walk into an exhibit and see them.

The whole experience went by in a flash. On an expedition like that, in the middle of the ocean, you don't do anything but work because that's all there is to do. Nothing to distract you. You are laser-focused. I loved that focus, I loved the work, and I loved what we were doing. I remember thinking, *I don't want to go home. I could stay out here forever and continue to dive every day and be in this bubble.* But that's exactly what it was. A bubble. It wasn't reality.

It was selfish to want to stay there. In many ways, the whole journey was somewhat selfish, to just leave my newly-wed husband behind. But I had really wanted to do it, so I did. And now, it was time to get back to the real world.

That said, if I hadn't been married, or if circumstances within the company hadn't been as volatile—which I will explain in a moment—I absolutely think I would have carried on doing the dives. I would have gone again if they'd asked me. It's terrible to say that when you realize all that's at stake. My husband recently asked, "If they came to you tomorrow, would you do it again?" Even now, I would have to say, "Absolutely."

***

After the expedition was over, reentry into the real world was hard. Not just because our bubble had abruptly popped but because two days after my second dive, there was a coup within the company. My boss, Mike Harris, had had to leave the expedition early due to family issues. That meant we had to finish the expedition without our leader, which was difficult enough. Then we found out that while we had been out at sea, there had been a hostile takeover of the company. Mike had gained his current position via a hostile takeover, and now someone else was doing the same thing to him.

I could not believe it. Not only was my mentor gone, but the leadership of the company was changing hands. All the hard work, all the positive media attention, all the restoring of artifacts and sharing them with survivors, family members, and the public—to come home to uncertainty and volatility within the company. Would I even have a job when I went back? I had just worked my ass off. How could this happen?

As if my uncertain professional future were not enough, our journey home was met with more hurricanes on-site and dangerously violent seas. It made the trip back to the states a stressful one to say the least. By the time I finally made it home, I was so tired. The stress had taken its toll, and I lost a lot of weight. To top it all off, we learned that the company's new leadership had closed down our offices in Clearwater, Florida and moved them to Atlanta. It felt like the final nail in the coffin.

I'd had this amazing experience, but coming home really was not what I had envisioned. Instead of a triumphant return, we were facing all these challenges—torn from the serenity of the ocean floor and flung into chaos. It almost felt like everything I'd done had been for nothing. It was a difficult lesson to learn that no one is impervious to change. The company did keep me on for six more months because they needed somebody to carry out the shows. Then, I was out.

However, in true from tragedy to triumph fashion, there was a wonderful silver lining in the fall of 2002. I was fortunate enough to have been sponsored for membership into the world re-nowned Explorer's Club in New York by my friend and fellow 2000 Expedition explorer, Dave Concannon. Dave is an attorney and explorer with an international legal practice representing sports equipment manufacturers, adventurers and explorers. He is a Vice President of The Explorers Club in New York City, in charge of expedition-related activities and honors awarded by the Club. David is a veteran of several deep-diving expeditions, including three expeditions to the R.M.S. Titanic.

From 2010 to 2013, David organized and led the expeditions that found and recovered the Apollo F-1 engines that launched men to the moon. What an incredible honor to be inducted into an international multidisciplinary professional society dedicated to the advancement of field research and the ideal that it is vital to preserve the instinct to explore. I was joining fellow explorers Neil Armstrong, Sally Ride and Dr. Sylvia Earle who became the first woman inducted in 1981. This induction was and still is a bittersweet reminder of what I accomplished and that with great reward comes great risk.

Fate of the Titanic

The biggest lesson I learned working in the for-profit world was that everyone is replaceable—for any reason and at any time. And with great reward comes great risk. This was the reality of business. This was the cutthroat world of shareholders, bottom lines, and hostile takeovers, and it was not fun being on the losing side. Keep in mind, I was an art student! No one had prepared me for these kinds of harsh lessons. Since then, it has been interesting and heartbreaking to watch the aftermath.

The original intent was always to create a permanent museum because traveling exhibitions take a toll on the artifacts. The museum was planned to be located in New York City, where the ship was meant to arrive. But the way things have played out instead is just a sad tale.

The company I worked for, RMS Titanic, Inc., was formed in 1987 and conducted eight expeditions to the *Titanic*, each costing upwards of $5 million. The reason I was brought onboard was to change the perception that the people in our company were graverobbers. The goal was to legitimize our work and start positioning our company to create exhibits in science museums versus traveling shows and exhibit halls. But that was not easy. A lot of universities did not want to work with us to conserve artifacts stateside.

Some of the artifacts we recovered from outside the ship had to be turned over to the courts in Norfolk, Virginia, who were required by law to conserve the artifacts and share them with the public. In my opinion, everything recovered from the *Titanic* should be curated and placed in a permanent museum. But this is a for-profit venture, not a nonprofit, meaning that investors are trying to make the most possible money. As of 2017, the entire *Titanic* collection is currently up for sale. The laws state that the items can never be sold separately; the collection has to be sold in its entirety.

There is still so much more down there to recover, but there remains a salvage block by the courts stipulating that you can't take a manned vehicle inside the ship. You can go inside with a remotely operated vehicle (ROV), which is how they collected footage for James Cameron's movie *Ghosts of the Abyss*. But you are not allowed to take anything off the ship or remove anything from the inside.

So many lives were affected by the *Titanic* expeditions, mine included. A lot of buyouts, a lot of takeovers, a lot of money spent, and many families destroyed. Over the years, George Tulloch—the former president and CEO who had been ousted by Mike Harris—died from a long battle with cancer. Ralph White, who I dove with on my first dive, passed away as well, along with many others. Sometimes, it felt like some sort of curse.

In 2017, it was announced that Premier Exhibitions (formerly RMS Titanic, Inc.) would be closing and attempting to sell the collection in its entirety. Now, instead of being displayed in a museum, this expansive collection of artifacts—these pieces of history—will go to the highest bidder. It will be interesting to see what happens with the artifacts and where the story of *Titanic* ends.

Chapter 4

Believe in Yourself

"Never ever give up"

——UNKNOWN

I came back from the *Titanic* with an uncertain future. I still had a restraining order against my father. I was newly married—a challenge all its own—and things became increasingly strained in the days after I returned from sea. There were so many questions. What would happen to my marriage? What would happen with my job? Where was my career going?

This was not the first time I would be disappointed by life's twists and turns, and it certainly would not be the last. Traveling, working with precious artifacts from the around the world, diving the wreck of the *Titanic*—these were incredible things I had been lucky enough to experience, but I could never truly appreciate any of them because of everything else going on at the time.

Jumping the queue is not about taking the easy road. It's about creating your own path, holding your head high, and tuning out the noise. It has taught me to wake up every morning and focus my thoughts on exactly what I am going to do that day. I know where my time is going to be spent, and when I go to bed every night, I think, *what was my impact on the world? What do I want it to be tomorrow?* I do this every single day. Was I kind to somebody? Did I show appreciation? Did I give the attention that was needed to my kids? Did I make a difference?

Uncharted Waters

My next job was working at the Gulf Coast Museum of Art. I was there for about two years in the capacity of community relations and was working for a museum director who was well-known and respected in the state of Florida.

We have a saying in museums when it comes to directors. "You're either there to build a museum, to build bridges, or to build programs." At the Gulf Coast Museum of Art, my boss's specialty was building the museums and programs—what he was not so good at was sustaining those museums. He tended to build them and move on, leaving them in financial straits.

This museum was a brand new, 65,000-square-foot facility in Largo. I was brought in to start cultivating relationships and to eventually start an endowment campaign because they hadn't put the annual income streams in place to sustain it, and memberships alone would not be enough. This was my first foray into fundraising, and I had an incredible mentor in Lloyd Horton, the chief fundraiser for All Children's Hospital in St. Petersburg.

Eventually, we learned that my boss, this well-known museum director, was abdicating his fundraising duties. He didn't see it as his job. He was making no effort to do things that would ultimately sustain the museum he directed.

Lloyd recommended that if I wanted to be a director of an art museum someday, I needed to temporarily step out of this field. The museum environment did not foster fundraisers, so fundraising was an invaluable skill that museum directors lacked. He told me to go cut my teeth somewhere in organizational health, at a university, or within a national organization. He recommended really understanding how to raise money, because the face of the new director for a museum would be somebody who took an active role in that capacity.

(As an aside, Lloyd would turn out to be right about this. These days, any CEO for a nonprofit, no matter where you are, is expected to be a skilled and experienced fundraiser. Back in 2002, most people in museum director roles didn't have practical fundraising experience. They might have the operational or programmatic side, but they didn't know how to raise money, nor did they want to learn.)

I took Lloyd's advice and left the Gulf Coast Museum of Art. I ended up taking a job with the National MS Society in a fundraising role. These were uncharted waters for me, but I had the big picture in mind. It was difficult for me to step out of the field that I knew and loved. I was a good curator. I could bring in big shows. But I also knew that I wanted to learn the administrative and human resources side of things and someday run a museum. That had always been the goal since I was 17, and I needed the experience to make that happen. So, I went after it.

***

By 2004, I was not in my "field" or even doing something remotely comfortable such as fundraising, but I was learning new skills. My first son had been born, and I was still struggling with the fragile relationship with my father. We would talk on the phone once in a while or meet two or three times a year, in a public place, but he was not the same person. Ultimately, a fear that I shared with my mother and sister came true. He committed suicide.

My father was on medication for the mania, but medication is simply not going to work if you are getting high, taking painkillers, and drinking alcohol. Eventually, his health severely deteriorated and his liver started to fail. He had to wear catheters and really couldn't deal with his body deteriorating. He spent a few years going from hospital to hospital, abusing the system. Then one day—I'll never forget it—I was coming home from Orlando when my husband called me on my cell phone.

"I need you to come straight home," he said. He wouldn't tell me anything else.

When I arrived home, there was a man standing beside my husband. I didn't know who this person was. It turned out to be an undercover police officer. He was there to tell me that my father had committed suicide. He had jumped off the balcony of the Guest Quarters Hotel in Tampa. The officer had gotten my name and address from the restraining order in the system. Strangely, my father had left his wallet in his room, containing a thousand dollars in cash. All I could think about was how bad I felt for the people who saw him do it. The people in the hotel who discovered him. They will live with that for the rest of their lives.

In my mind, his suicide was a selfish act. I always think of the people left behind and the damage it does to their lives. My father left three grandsons behind. I was the one who had to tell my sister and mother what happened, and even though my sister was the executor for the estate, she did not have the emotional capacity to assist with the arrangements. I took care of everything. The cost to cremate him and his final preparations at Florida National Cemetery in Bushnell totaled one thousand dollars, the same amount he had left in his wallet. One of the last things he did, I learned, was to walk across the street and cash a thousand-dollar check at Amscot Financial. We had to go to his rental house and clean his things out. He had filed for bankruptcy years ago, so everything was paid in cash. It was a clean departure.

I don't feel anger when I think of my father, I just think, *What a waste*. The truth is, for me, I mourned the loss of my father many years before his death. It was not the act of his suicide that provided the finality; it was the process of creating boundaries, a structure of safety, and ultimately a healthier life that allowed me to be free and uncontrolled to this day.

A lot of people deal with alcoholism, verbal abuse, and mental illness. I realize I am not special because I had to deal with these issues. However, I also realize that dealing with them made all the difference in how I moved forward.

To this day, I continue to move forward and not allow the past to dictate my present. It is because of this adversity that I empathize with the nonprofits I serve. This same empathy fuels me to ensure that any individual has access to the support need to move beyond their current circumstances, because I am living proof it can make all the difference between a functioning or nonfunctioning person in society.

CEO at Age 30

After two years working fundraising within the profession—building my toolkit and acquiring the skills I needed—I received a call from one of the board members at the Gulf Coast Museum of Art who was about to separate employment with the existing director. He wanted to see if I was interested in applying.

I learned that after I left the Gulf Coast Museum of Art, the director I had been working for did not continue to raise money. If he had built the appropriate pipeline of financial support, things would have been fine. Instead, he continued to plunder the endowment for operations, which is a funding source you should only take when funding times are lean.

I knew that if I took this job, I would be a CEO at age thirty *and* the youngest museum director in the state of Florida. I also knew that the museum was struggling financially, meaning there was a possibility that it would close, and if it did, the closure would happen under my leadership. But this was something I had wanted for a long time. I thought if I could lead the museum through this crisis and get it to survive, it would demonstrate my strong leadership skills.

I knew this challenge was going to take everything I had developed so far. If I was victorious in the face of all my critics, I would create a new model for successful leadership. I felt I could do it, even though it was going to be an uphill battle. I had the confidence, and now I had the fundraising experience. Plus, I was going back to a community that was like a second home to me. I decided to take the job.

When I accepted the job, I was pregnant with my second child ... but we hadn't told anyone yet. I thought, *Youngest museum director, CEO, pregnant, and no one knows.*

Well, here we go.

Chapter 5

Make Your Health a Priority

"The first wealth is health."
—Ralph Waldo Emerson

knew that there were two possible paths going into the museum director position. I was either going to set them up for a merger, or I was going to set them up to be successful but perhaps at a different location.

The museum had debt from ten years prior of around a million dollars on the books that the former director never paid down. I went through the staff, assembled the right team, and tried to sift through the board and put together a business plan.

As part of my plan, I contacted the city and said, "We're on your property, but you did nothing to make us successful. You have not marketed us. The road was under construction for years and people couldn't get to us." As a result, they agreed to let us pay down the debt in three installments, as long as we were showing that we were bringing in more mainstream shows to attract more public in to start fundraising.

I worked tirelessly, day and night. I did not miss one day of work, ever, the entire time I was there. My feet would hit the ground, and every day I felt invigorated and passionate about the task in front of me. I successfully reduced just under a million dollars of debt and fully paid off within my first eight months on the job. The next step was to move to a new location. We could not afford to stay in the current facility in Largo because we could not sustain the cost of maintaining the campus and were not getting the foot traffic we needed. My goal was to move the museum to Clearwater, Florida.

I worked with the City of Clearwater, and the city agreed to give us an old bank building right downtown. We could rehab it and get the expenses under control. The city even agreed to pay our moving expenses and the first couple months of rent. We began the process of brokering a deal on the space. All we had to do was have our current building appraised and then sell it to the city of Largo. I knew enough to grease the wheels. I knew how to work the system. I was not sure whether it was going to happen or not, but we asked them to buy the building so we could use that money to move and survive, put the funds into an endowment, and start small.

Pregnancy, Childbirth, and the Working Woman

Things were happening at a fast pace, I was working hard, and was beginning to think, *I might actually pull this off!* It was around this time that I went in for a routine prenatal checkup. With both my children, I had a treatment called a cervical cerclage. It's a small stitch to keep your cervix shut so you don't miscarry. I had already had that procedure once without any complications. This time was different.

After the examination, I was told that in order to ensure the health of the baby, they needed to put me on bed rest.

I looked at her. "*Bed rest?*"

I thought they were going to take out the stitch. They usually do that, and then the baby comes when it's going to come.

"We can't take the stitch out," she said, "and the baby is not mature enough to be able to live on its own if you were to give birth. There is too much pressure because you are on your feet too much. You're going to have to be put on bed rest for the next two months. Then we'll take out the cerclage, and you can go back to work."

Two months? Was she kidding? I couldn't be on two months of bed rest!

This wasn't just a two-month sentence either, because once you remove the stitch, it means the baby is going to come within a week. She was telling me I needed to stop working for two months, then I could go back to work for maybe a week, and then I'd have the baby.

I said, "Well, when? Okay, maybe Monday. I can do that because I have to go back and sign payroll, and...."

"No, you don't understand," she said. "You are on bed rest *now*. You're not going back to work."

What?

I looked at her and said, "There's no way." I looked at my husband. "There's no way!"

But Eric knew. He held his head down and reached out for my hand and said "Michelle, you can't."

I left there thinking, *Maybe I can sneak into work tomorrow and get some minimal things done, at least.* Eric did not like that idea. In the end, I realized there was no fighting it.

I remember having to call the board and break the news. They knew there was no other choice, and nobody is going to make you pick your job over the health of your baby, but I still felt like I was being judged.

No one said it, but I felt like they were thinking "Typical. This is what we get for hiring this young woman." That's how I felt. That has always been a stigma against the working female, and make no mistake, it is still alive and well today. Because this is still the real world.

I did what I needed to do. This was the first of several lessons regarding the importance of health. It was also a lesson in learning that the sacrifices and compromises of being a mother begin for a woman long before delivery.

Health Comes First

I know it might sound like a cliché, but my advice is that you need to put your health first. For highly motivated working women, it's easy to forget that. It is easy to reach a point where you just keep going and going.

When you're a young woman like I was—first-time director, first time in leadership—you are continuously sacrificing. You have a lot to prove, so you're constantly going the extra mile. You're trying to impress people. And then something jars that.

Fortunately, I was smart enough to know that this was one of those moments where I had to make the right choice. I was not going to be Superwoman here. I had to do what was best not only for the health of the baby but also for myself.

While on bed rest, I was allowed to be on my feet for only thirty minutes a day. I could take a shower or maybe get up to go eat. I wasn't even allowed to sit up. I already had a three-year-old son at home, so now I am in bed, and my husband is a single parent. And I have to rely on people—which, as you know, is really hard for a control freak. To top it all off, I had to figure out now how to run an art museum, which was potentially going downhill, from my bedside. (This was 2007. It was not the remote work environment. We weren't there yet.)

I did what I had to do. I set everything up from home. I set up my office from my bedside. I'd work every day lying on my back. I had a staff person who lived near me who would bring me the mail every day and deliver the checks to sign and take to my mailbox. That was my life for two months.

Finally, they took the stitch out, and I went back to work. A week later, I was in a finance meeting and started to feel pain. My CFO said, "You might be in labor. Maybe you should go home." She was right.

When we arrived at the hospital, the doctor told me I had a choice: either I could induce immediately because I was at high-risk, or I could go home, but I would most likely be back at the hospital within forty-eight hours.

I said, "I have my mom at home watching Matthew for as long as we need her. Let's do this."

As they were prepping me to give birth, I suddenly looked at my watch and noticed the date. I started crying. Eric looked at me, confused. I said, "Eric, today is the day my father died. I can't possibly have my son's birthday be on the same day my father died."

Eric said to the doctor, "Can you just give us a minute?"

We had the room to ourselves, I cried for a minute. Finally, Eric said, "Do you want to wait? It's 10:30 at night. Do you think you can wait two hours?"

I thought about that for a minute. "You know what?" I said. "Nope. We're going to do this now. I'm not going to give him the power." I was not going to give my father any more control over my life. If anything, this was going to be a positive day. Eric called the doctor back in, and I said, "Let's go."

I was in labor for the longest time with my first child. We named him Matthew, which means "Gift of the Lord." He was difficult to deliver and stayed in the NICU for four weeks. But the second one, it was like I coughed and we were done. His birthday is October 4th, the same day my father had died three years earlier. We named him Nicholas Alexander, the strongest Greek name I knew, because he had been through so much.

Do I dwell on the fact that Nicholas's birthday was the same day my father died? No. If anything, I'm glad, because now I think of that day as my son's birthday. Since then, I really have never thought about it as the day my father died.

I went back to work, and Nicholas came with me every day. He is sleeping in a baby sling while I'm curating art exhibits. What are you going to do? He sleeps and poops and eats a bottle. I'm good. I got this.

I felt blessed and humbled beyond relief. Two healthy sons, a dream job, a supportive husband, and a newfound perspective on life.

***

Christmas came two months later, and the City of Largo held a county-commission vote on whether to purchase the museum buildings from us. This was the big moment; my whole plan hinged on this decision. If they allowed us to sell the buildings, I could use the sale from the property to move the museum to smaller location to rebuild the endowment and programs.

My good friend and county commissioner called me at home on Christmas break in 2008. He said, "Michelle, we're not going to vote to buy the building. We just don't have the money to do it."

"Okay," I said. "Can you amend the lease? Then at least we could sell it to somebody else."

"We're not going to do that either," he said.

The writing was on the wall. The city didn't have to buy the building, and they didn't have to allow us to sell it, either. But, if we closed, they would get the buildings free and clear. They were leveraging our failing museum to get a free building.

"Okay," I said. "Then you've just closed a museum and Pinellas County cultural jewel with over 75 years of history."

That was devastating.

In late January of 2008, the membership of the Museum voted to close the museum and then subsequently the Board of Trustees voted to dissolve the Museum. I remember coming home that day reminding myself that a community will support what it ultimately wants and that despite my best effort, the community did not support this institution once it was moved to a location with virtually no presence. This lesson has stuck with me — the importance of location and community support.

I hired a company to handle the PR because I could not deal with the press on my own. I had inherited all these problems from my predecessor. Chances had always been slim that the museum could be saved, but, nevertheless, it was on *my* watch that the Gulf Coast Museum of Art closed after seventy-five years of operation.

I was able to close the museum down in a respectful way. The hard part was knowing that I had to now separate our collection to other museums. The Salvador

Dalí Museum and the Tampa Museum both came to me, wanting our collection. All I wanted to do was shut the door and hide.

I received a phone call from one of the county commissioners who did not vote to close the museum. Two of the commissioners and the president of St. Petersburg College, had a proposition for me. They offered to take the whole Gulf Coast Museum collection and put it with the college so it could be kept in Pinellas County where it belonged. The foundation would take it over and display the collection in the Leepa-Rattner Museum of Art and other places.

I thought, *Oh my God, that's such a great solution!* But what I said was, "Well, are there any jobs that I can transition for my staff?"

I was able to get four jobs for my staff. They offered me a job, too, but I didn't take it. I was done. My CFO and I stayed until the end. We each received a severance and took a couple of months off. I had given it everything I had, and now, I had nothing left.

Since this experience, I have been approached by many leaders whose organizations were on the brink of closing and, ironically, reached out to me for advice. As painful as it was to be known as the leader at the helm during this change, I always took the call and counseled these people as best I could. Why? Because no one was there to counsel me when I needed it or wanted to be associated with a closing venture.

There were three things I learned from my experience that I impart when asked. When you are in a dire situation:

1. Focus on the things that matter, not the distractors
   a. Hone things down to what you really *need* to do

2. Assemble a support team
   b. Choose a team of people who have the right skill sets to get you through the transition

3. Share your experience with others
   c. Remain humble and shine a light for others

To this day, when I run into people who walked through that tough time with me, it is not the closure they bring up; it is the character and grace for which I am commended. I still have the cards and letters I received during this difficult time as a reminder that someone is always watching how a leader responds to adversity. That is something I cherish because I would not have thought, at thirty-six years old, that I would have been able to embody those attributes during such a difficult time. I have tried to maintain these characteristics throughout my career and have found people respond to this far better than the alternative: placing blame on others or leaving things in flames. It was my first lesson of how I would want to be remembered as a leader, even in crisis.

Sh*t Sandwich Opportunities

I learned later in life that a lot of women do what I did while I was still a museum director—They see an opportunity to achieve a big goal or a dream, and even if it's not the best situation, they go for it.

Many professional women do not want to pass on an opportunity that comes their way because they don't know when, or if, such an opportunity will come up again. Instead of seeing a hopeless situation that should be avoided, they say, "I can do it. I'm the person for the job. I'm going to come in and save it." Whatever "it" is.

I never judge female leaders, now that I've been in a similar position. There are more women in leadership roles today than ever before, but in many ways, *attitudes* toward women in leadership roles have stayed the same. We are judged more harshly, and every decision we make, professionally or personally, is heavily scrutinized.

Marissa Mayer, the former president and CEO of Yahoo, was judged harshly for how soon she went back to work after her pregnancy. Mary Barra, the chairman and CEO of General Motors, took the job and walked into a fiasco. Women tend to be given opportunities that are inherently bad situations—nearly hopeless scenarios—and then blamed when it doesn't work out.

We are eager to prove ourselves, so we are the ones who step up, step in, and take the bullet. We don't get to say what an opportunity looks like when it shows up. Usually, we are tossed a sh*t sandwich and told, "Here, you fix it now." All we can do is our best work.

My museum director opportunity was not the one I wanted, but I took it anyway. The experience was a humbling lesson. It was definitely not the experience I had wanted so badly and did not turn out at all the way I thought it would. It's something I still struggle with, but I still wouldn't change the decision I made to go after it.

I know I did everything I could to save that museum. When it didn't work out, I at least tried to handle it in a graceful way. I was able shut the doors with dignity, and there was money left over to put in an endowment for the conservation of the artifacts as they went on. Plus, I tried to find jobs for people and provide some stability for those whose lives had been shaken by the closure.

At the time, it was difficult to see the silver lining in any of this, but after the recession of 2008, many organizations were in a similar place and a lot of leaders found themselves in the same position I had been in just a few years prior. You'd be surprised how many calls I get, even to this day, saying, "We're on the verge of closing. We didn't make the right hire." Why do they call me? Because they know my history. Who better equipped to help them through it?

I was always happy to help. I felt that by offering support in this area, it was a way to be a different type of colleague—vulnerable, open, and empathetic. It became the impetus for me to start the consulting company I run today. I don't want nonprofits to experience the kind of misfortune I went through. It was devastating and embarrassing at the time, but, then again, the only reason any of this happened is because my story was so public. In order for others to know you are the best person for the job, you have to become comfortable telling your story and not be embarrassed by it.

The Battle Against Stress and the True Cost of Leadership

Stress shows itself in interesting ways. I meet women and men all the time—and read stories about many individuals—whose personal lives suffer the adverse effects of their professional roles. Whether it's their marriages, physical health, or mental health, the costs associated with high levels of stress are very real. Through my museum director job, I learned the importance of taking care of yourself.

For three years I had been working every day loving what I did, but I never relaxed. After the museum closed, I had six to eight months where the stress was still coming out of my body. My body responded to the level of stress I had been experiencing. I was diagnosed with Crohn's disease and a blood deficiency. There is no history of Crohn's in my family, so I personally feel that this was brought on by stress and will be the way my body continues to respond to stress. And my body never recouped. I manage it to this day. I get infusions at home every eight weeks to be healthy and to manage the Crohn's.

Often, the impact of stress doesn't appear right away. It compounds over time. It might even be ten years down the road. Then suddenly, there is a huge impact. It may not manifest as an ailment like it did in me. Other people eat. Other people drink. Other people might choose to do drugs, like my father. Then there are those who take it to the opposite extreme: they over-exercise or are hyper-controlling about their food intake and end up hurting themselves. In their pursuit of stress relief, they turn a healthy habit into an unhealthy one.

I do feel fortunate that I learned the lesson of taking care of my health in my thirties, because I've never since had that imbalance again. It was a tough lesson, but if I hadn't gone through it, I would not have come out with the model I eventually developed as an entrepreneur.

Everything I've done since was done in order to put things into perspective:

- How am I going to balance this with my family?

- How am I going to balance my health in order to be the best me, of service to my clients and realistic in my goals and dreams?

Have you ever seen side-by-side photos of presidents at the start their presidency vs. when they leave office? The change is remarkable. You can see the physical toll the job has taken on them and how much they have aged.

Not enough is said or written about the toll that stress takes on your health, your body, and your relationships. There's nothing wrong with hard work, but you have to know when to draw the line. You have to be able to step back and say, "I've done my best. I have put in enough hours at work this week."

Part of leadership is knowing how to handle your health. If you are reading this and have not found that balance yet, I'd like to offer some strategies for what you can do if you find yourself burning the candle at both ends.

1. Set Clear Goals

There is no doubt in my mind that my upbringing had a huge role in the way I set goals. Goals provided *structure*. We were constantly walking on eggshells in my house. There was no routine no structure and no sense of normalcy. I've accomplished my goals in my adult life because, number one, they were things I truly wanted to do, and number two, because it provided the structure I needed.

Establishing the goals you want to accomplish professionally and personally is essential. Make it a priority to do this each year. Ask yourself, "What are my top three priorities of the year?"

We tend to naturally think of our goals in terms of years—New Year's resolutions, five-year plans—but you have to break your goals down into smaller increments. When it comes to weight or body image, for example, you can set a big goal for the end of the year, but real progress occurs on a much smaller level. Overachievers like me set big goals, sometimes to our own detriment. Start by breaking your big goals down into small, actionable steps that can be implemented on a day-to-day basis.

2. Plan Your Day

To this day, people ask, "Were there any repercussions from your childhood?" I'm proud to say that I didn't have unhealthy relationships, but my need for structure, my need to plan things, comes from a lifetime of growing up in an unstructured, haphazard, unreliable setting with an alcoholic parent. On the plus side, rigorous planning has allowed me to achieve big goals and live a fulfilled life. I know that the reason I was able to accomplish a lot of my goals at a young age was because staying focused and having a structure was comforting and necessary for me.

On a day-to-day basis, map out your day. Based on what your life looks like and what you ultimately want to achieve—whether it's exercise, career, kids, etc.—where does that all fit into *this day*? Ask yourself:

- What are the true priorities for this day?

- What progress can I make today towards my larger goals?

Progress doesn't just happen. You have to plan for it, and at some point, chaos will catch up.

As controversial as this may sound, you have to be selfish. Put yourself first. If you're suffering, you're no good to anybody.

3. Track Your Time

If you find planning your day to be difficult, it may be because you have a problem with the concept of planning. When I coach my clients, I tell them to start by working on a time management chart. I know it's a pain in the ass, but before you can decide how to establish change, you need to see where your time is currently being spent. Track both your work hours and your personal time. What does your time sheet look like on a day-to-day and week-to-week basis? How much are you spending on family time, workout time, business time, and so on.

We all have a notion of how we spend our time, but that notion is frequently off the mark. People are surprised to find out how they're *actually* spending their days. By tracking your time, you quickly learn what things you *should* you be working on every day that you're not. You can also identify the things you currently spend time on during your workday that you should be allocating or delegating to somebody else. Ask yourself, "Is this task really where I want to be spending my time?" If not, have someone else do it. This will get you to the point where you're (1) prioritizing things for your health and mental well-being, and (2) prioritizing the right things for your current purpose.

Delegating tasks means you will have to get comfortable with giving up control, but this frees up your time for the things you should be focusing on. It also reduces the accumulation of stress so you don't burn out, which lowers your risk for health issues and will safeguard the love and passion you feel for your job.

 # TIME MANAGEMENT CHART

DIRECTIONS: Record your daily activities and how much time they take, including the weekend. Use a different color for each activity (e.g. eating, sleeping, travel to & from work, meetings, emails, workouts, leisure).

	Monday	Tuesday	Wednesday	Thursday	Friday	Saturday	Sunday
12 AM							
1							
2							
3							
4							
5							
6							
7							
8							
9							
10							
11							
12 PM							
1							
2							
3							
4							
5							
6							
7							
8							
9							
10							
11							

You can't fix an imbalance between your work life and home life (or health life) until you see it. A lot of people simply don't understand how they created their current predicament. A time study allows you see where your time is going. It shines a light on your daily routine and gives you a clear picture of what your life looks like. It is often a painful exercise, but it's an essential step.

Where is Your "Soft Place" to Fall?

You must have mechanisms in place to prevent burnout *before* it strikes. For some people, this means waking up early and working out. For others, it's more about meditation and spiritual peace. Some people write in journals. Some people simply need to be home, in a safe space, with family or friends who love them unconditionally and can help them recharge and refill their cup.

The question is, how long do you want to keep doing what you're currently doing? Do you want to burn yourself out to the point where it's not fun anymore, or you become so stressed that you have nothing left to give? Our culture places a higher value on work time than "me" time. But if you don't prioritize me time once in a while, you *will* burn out, and the work time will slowly kill you.

Examples of "Me" Time:

- Create time every day or every week just for you

- Go offline for the weekend—no computer, no email, no thinking about work

- Create a getaway: a girl's weekend, a spa day, wine tour, or some beach time

  There are ways to do this inexpensively that will recharge your spirit without taking a toll on your pocketbook:

- Use your sick days and personal days

- Set aside a percentage of your paycheck exclusively to save for a vacation

- If you're the kind of person who gets re-energized by quiet time at home, make it a "staycation"

If you are reading this book and are already at the point of severe burnout, simply adding me time to your schedule might not cut it. My suggestion is to take some time off.

If things get bad enough, I think a millennial woman with her priorities in order will probably leave her job. But if you love your job and want to stay, but just don't know how, ask yourself how you can take some meaningful time off. Can you take a sabbatical and clear your head to think about the next step? You may not be in the financial position to do that, but it might be the best thing you could do for yourself. You are going to have to pause at some point because if you don't, you will hit rock bottom.

Rock bottom varies from person to person, but it always shows itself somewhere. If it starts to show at work, you could lose your job. If it starts to show in your daily habits, your health will suffer. If it shows itself at home, you will have problems in your marriage. And if you're not present as a parent, your kids will suffer.

A board member I knew once shared his story of burnout with me. He told me, "My wife has a saying. You cannot be all sunshine and lightness all day at work and then darkness at night at home." In other words, you can't give 100 percent at the office, then come home and default to zero. It's not fair to be your best self at work, then come home and be difficult to your family and be so burned out that you go to bed after dinner without asking anybody about their day.

The questions to ask yourself now are:

- What level of stress am I at?

- What caused this stress?

- What is at risk if I continue at this level of stress and depletion?

Perhaps most importantly, ask yourself: From where do I derive my happiness?

Personally, I love what I do for a living, but that doesn't mean it's *all* I want to do. There's so much joy in the balance of a good workout at 5:00 a.m. or spending one-on-one time with my kids. If you don't pay attention, those things can slip through the cracks. It comes down to understanding where you're spending your time, what's sucking the energy out of your life, and how it's manifesting.

Not everyone wants to get up at five in the morning to work out. I get that. It's not about changing who you are. It's about doing what works for you. What is relaxing to you? How do you have fun? Is it reading books? Is it riding horses? Going for a walk? Cooking? Traveling? Dancing? What do *you* love to do?

When I find that a person isn't doing anything for themselves to feed their soul, that is a big problem. The best thing you can do for yourself is to discover—or rediscover—the personal passion that feeds your soul. Find it and don't lose it!

Being present for your colleagues or clients—being present for your family, being present so you can enjoy what you're doing—is one of the main ways I know of to maintain balance.

Although it's been a lot easier to maintain the balance since I started my own business, I still have to manage my Crohn's and I am more open with those who suffer from it as it is a part of me but not the sum of me. I also pick projects I *want* to do, as opposed to consultants who take everything that comes their way because they're worried they won't get the next gig. I've never really had that thought in my mind. I have the exact opposite mindset. If

I like the project and see an opportunity to help, I tend to say "yes" and then figure out how to do it later. Then I'll sit down and map out how many hours it will take with each client to accomplish this. Because I know that every hour will directly affect my health and my family time.

Exercise: Self-Care

1. Make a list of ways you can care for yourself today.
2. What passions would you like to spend more time on or rediscover?
3. How can you insert some "me" time into your schedule do this week? This month?

Chapter 6

Make the Jump and Create a New Roadmap

"If you don't build your dreams, someone will hire you to help build theirs."

—Tony Gaskin

By the time I was thirty-six, my CEO position had come to an end, and I had no clue what to do next.

I had always been a goal-setter, and for the first time in my life, I didn't have a trajectory firmly established. For the next couple of years, I went back into the fundraising role, purposely declining CEO and leadership roles. I wanted to take a step back, accept the health lesson, and give myself time to regroup.

During this time, a shift occurred. Because of everything I'd been through, I started to become a leader in this area, with individuals seeking guidance and mentorship. It was the first time I felt I had a skill set that people wanted to learn; I was in a position where I could teach and help people, and I wouldn't have the pressures I'd had to deal with in the past.

It was my first venture into mentoring, both of which would soon become important parts of my career.

Going Against the Grain

At the time, I was working at a comfortable job. I took it knowing that I was on track for another leadership role—possibly even taking over as the CEO when he left. But after fielding so many questions from colleagues, navigating people issues similar to those I had faced, the idea of creating a full-time career out of consulting began to feel like an increasingly feasible way to move forward in my professional life. I would get the variety I wanted in my work life, and the focus would be on fixing problems and moving from project to project, serving as a partner to leaders who were struggling with many of the issue I had faced.

For about six months, I interviewed a lot of female nonprofit consultants who I knew in the area, and I devised a list of questions. I would ask them things like:

- Why did you decide on your niche?

- How do you get your business?

- How did you position yourself as an authority in your area?

- How have you sustained yourself in your field?

- What are the pitfalls of what you do?

- What were the lessons you learned?

Then I started looking at myself, my track record, and my personality. I asked myself, "What do I struggle with the most?"

My conclusion was that I was somebody who wanted to come into a company or a situation for three years or so, fix a problem(s), and then move on. I have a certain amount of energy, and by now, I had learned that what I did took *a lot* of energy. Not everybody is built that way. Many maintain or fix what is comfortable for them, and leave the areas alone that they do not understand, until the next leader comes along. Based on what was out there, I realized that I was well-positioned to start my own business. This was how I would position myself as no one else had what I was offering.

CASE STUDY: Interviewing for a Position

The choice to strike out on my own was not a decision I arrived at lightly. I had determined that running my own business was where I belonged. Whether you're starting your own business, attempting to make it as a self-employed contractor, or making a transition from an old employer to a new job, it's sometimes hard to discern whether or not you are a good fit for a particular job or role. How do you discover the setting that's a good fit for you?

You can study and research all you want, but when it comes right down to it, part of it is trial and error. Whatever your occupation, you have to discover firsthand where your skill sets are a good fit. These days, when interviewing for a position, don't expect to get the hackneyed "strengths and weaknesses" kinds of interview questions. Modern interviews are about digging down to do your morals and ethics. The interviewers' mission is to find out, does your personality fit here? Will you be a good fit within the team they have developed? Millennials are great at preparing and doing the research when they really want something, but you can't just Google, "top ten interview questions" and prepare some responses.

Many organizations are doing behavioral interviewing. The problem a lot of people run into in interviews is that they say what they think the other person wants to hear. But it's not easy to do that with behavioral interview questions. These are not simple questions.

Personally, when I interview people, I tell them, "This is the process. I'm going to ask you some standard questions to first qualify you with your qualities to determine if you're a match for the position. Then I am going to ask some deeper, not-so-standard questions." The intention is not to catch you off guard. The aim is to make you think about specific examples to get to the core of who you are.

I tend to ask questions like, Tell me about a time you had fire someone? What did you learn from the experience and what would you differently? I can find out very quickly who has really had that experience of sitting across the table from somebody and firing them. There is a big difference between, say, asking someone about their biggest failure and asking them *how they handle* failure. It's not scripted. It's not formulated. You have to give examples. You have to reveal things about yourself. You must reveal things about yourself because with behavioral interviewing, you only typically get to four or five questions in an hour. If you can't provide specific examples, it quickly reveals that you lack experience.

When I work with younger women who are interviewing for various opportunities, whether it's volunteerism or positions in the workplace, I always try to counsel them about this. I want them to be prepared for questions that dig down to the heart of who they really are and get comfortable with it. And remember: You're not just interviewing to fill a position. You're there to *join a team*.

You should never go to an interview with the mindset that you're just filling the duties listed in the description. At the end of the day, you can *create* whatever the job description says. The same goes for volunteering. If you have additional ambitions and skills to bring to the table, it will set you apart from the crowd.

Additionally, don't go in there with your shields up. Be more vulnerable in interviews. Talk about your failures and mistakes just as much as your accomplishments. This isn't just about what you can do. It's about who you are. When you get right down to it, what we're talking about is authenticity.

"On trust, it's really about authenticity and transparency. We live in a world where people can sense insincerity or corporate-speak from a mile away. Companies and leaders have to be authentic in tone, voice, and action. It's not just about "saying the right thing" but talking about what matters most to your company and your people, and backing that up with action.

On engagement, it's about purpose and meaningful work. It's finding assignments for people that stretch and challenge them, and make a real impact for our clients and our communities. It's making our people feel entrepreneurial and that they are making a difference. In our organization, you're literally one phone call away from being able to solve almost any problem that a client could face, in a way that I believe is really unique in the marketplace. That's an energizing prospect as you come to work every day!"

—CATHY ENGELBERT, CEO OF DELOITTE LLP

Making the Jump

I started this book with the story of how I left my current job to start my consulting business—when I told my boss I'd give him six months and he countered by giving *me* one. I had put myself out there, tried to be honest and fair, and this is what happened. I wasn't taking another job or going to a competitor. This was life-changing for me, but I had unintentionally offended this person.

I felt nervous about now only having one month. My business had been an idea up until that point. Six months would have been plenty of time to change my mind.

But *one month*?

This whole thing was suddenly very real. I had no idea how to start a business from scratch! Ultimately, I put on my big girl panties and hired some of the great people I had surrounded myself with in the past to fill in the knowledge gaps and help me move forward.

Ironically, once I started sharing my plan with people, people started calling me. While I was finishing up my job, I already had three contracts in the hopper. I hired my attorney to file all the paperwork. Here I was—at that time, I think I was making $90,000 a year—and my husband was worried about our finances.

Funny, I never even worried about that. I still don't. It turned out I didn't miss a beat financially, and my revenue doubled in the second year.

Chapter 7

Building A Business

"Your work is going to fill a large part of your life, and the only way to be truly satisfied is to do what you believe is great work. The only way to do great work is to love what you do."

—STEVE JOBS

D eveloping my business was an intentional process. I was all-in, and if I was going to give this a go, it wasn't going to be to just replace my income or "get by." I had been a CEO making over a hundred grand a year, and I did not intend to go backward.

I've met a lot of female entrepreneurs who are all-in like me; keeping the lights on and paying the mortgage is dependent on their success. But I've also met many female business owners and entrepreneurs who are, for lack of a better term, living off their husbands' incomes with no pressure to really produce. Everyone's situation is different. The key to navigating your path to success as a business owner is to know yourself, know your market, know your worth, and, perhaps most of all, understand that no matter what you are doing or selling, *you* are the product.

You Are the Product

When I first started taking clients, I realized, to my horror, that had nothing to show them! My website wasn't done. I didn't even have business cards yet. I didn't have a widget. I said to my husband, "I have a meeting with a client and I don't have *anything*!"

"You are the product," he told me. "It doesn't matter if you have the business cards. You're there to sell yourself and the value you bring to the table." I have never forgotten that.

Whether I'm in a room with somebody who is selling flip-flops or hair bands or a mobile app, I always remind myself that they are buying into me. I am the product. My look, my personality, my capabilities, my track record, and, most of all, my reputation and character. Those who continue to hire me for my services are buying into the quality of what I bring to the table.

No matter what sort of work you do, whether self-employed or otherwise, you *are* the business. And it's essential to know the value of your product. Everything in this chapter comes down to how to cultivate your product (you) to build a successful business.

Finding Your Purpose

If you are just starting out, you may not need business cards or a website, but you do need to spend some time planning. The first step is to ask yourself the following:

1. What do I like to do the most?

2. What do I like to do the least?

3. What am I not qualified to do (e.g., bookkeeping, taxes, payroll, distribution)?

4. What are my strengths?

5. What type of people do I like to work with?

The time I spent interviewing nonprofit consultants taught me one thing: I didn't want to be a consultant who was a paid staff member.

I had found that a lot of the consultants I dealt with weren't treating consulting like a full-time job. Many were part-time, or were okay with making an income of $40,000. Others were just looking to replace their existing income or had a specific dollar figure they need to make in order to meet their expenses. As long as they could make "x" amount per year and were working a forty-hour week, they were happy. When it came to those who were married, the husband was often the primary breadwinner and carried the health insurance, so the consulting paycheck was not the motivating factor. (My household is set up differently. It is a 50-50 partnership.)

I also knew I didn't want to spend all my time fundraising. There were already plenty of people out there fundraising, writing grants, putting together special events, and building capacity. However, based on my experience, you cannot build capacity without the proper infrastructure. Therefore, I created a model that had three areas that were necessary for nonprofits to thrive and survive: executive searches (hiring the right people), organizational management (sound infrastructure), and fundraising (securing the necessary resources to sustain a mission). I created a model that was built on my experience—literally!

Learn Your Worth

A lot of women find it challenging to transition from being an employee to building a business while still meeting their expenses. When it comes to financing, I recommend you look at all your options. Be realistic. Ask yourself, "How am I going to support myself?"

• Do I take a loan? What's available for small businesses?

• What is available to minority-owned and/or female-owned businesses?

- Do I pull from my savings and invest in myself?

- Do I remain conservative, wait until next year, and start putting money aside?

For me, when I started my business, I took $5,000 from *my* savings. That was it. Because if I was going to invest in anybody, it would be myself. My husband and I were fortunate enough to have built up our savings when we were younger, so the money was definitely there if I needed it. But I didn't want to touch it. I felt that if I used that as a crutch, I wouldn't be as aggressive. That was the best option for me, but your best option may look a little different. It's going to depend on your personality, what you're in tune with, what's at stake, and the level of risk you're comfortable taking.

You also must figure out your pricing points. I had the advantage of having hired consultants in the past, so I knew the market, and I knew who I was competing with. If you do not know your market, take the time to learn. You need to know how to defend the cost of your service and back it up with an hourly rate.

When you're first starting out, you will definitely have to take some clients you might not be thrilled about working with. I took a few jobs like that myself, but eventually, I had to do what was right for me. After all, what was the point of doing any of this if I didn't enjoy it? Sure, I was out to make a living, but the goal was also to have more control over what I was doing, who I was working with, and what was going to be fulfilling to me—having the power to pick and choose projects versus working for somebody.

It's been refreshing to be able to say "no" to undesirable projects, but that's not to say it's been easy. Each project is different. There are always going to be times when you are called on to step outside your comfort zone. You're going to have to work some extra hours and sink some hard time into your dream. When you go through that for the first time, it can be very difficult. But the second time, that's when you must ask yourself the following:

1. What am I going to learn from this?

2. What should I be doing differently?

3. What can I do better?

4. What do I need to reprioritize?
   (Be honest with yourself.)

You might have a pretty good idea of how many hours a task will take, but you should always build in some wiggle room. You have to be nimble, because things change. That's the nice thing about planning. If you have a somewhat clear idea in your head of what awaits, you can anticipate whether you might need to add in a few extra hours in case a client requires more of your time—or if a task is more labor-intensive than you anticipated or whatever the case might be.

I'm not above putting in extra elbow grease to meet the client's expectations, but we also need to agree to be flexible because I know my value. All my contracts include the cost per project, but I also include a clause that if we exceed "x" number of hours, I charge the following hourly rate. If they want something outside the scope of the immediate work or they want something I don't normally offer, I want to be able to help them without compromising my worth.

Many young women, feeling the pressure to produce great work and go above and beyond expectations, end up taking on so much extra work that they devalue their time—and themselves. That's the downside of wanting to prove yourself. It's essential to determine how much is enough, and when the extra work you're putting in merits extra compensation.

That's what it looks like to know your worth. It takes a while to establish this, to not underestimate it, and to not be scared to walk away if somebody doesn't value your worth.

Get Out There and Leverage Your Network

Putting in the effort to leverage your network and get your name out there is your responsibility, because the work isn't going to come to you.

Your clients are everywhere. Look at your current employer and realize they could eventually be a client. Ask former colleagues if they need any work done. I started by simply going to the people I had worked with before, the ones I trusted, and sharing my story. Get out there and network, no matter how long you have been in business.

I have learned to be smart about where I spend my time. I do not attend events where there isn't a decision maker or if it won't further my business in some way. Obviously, I am fishing in all the nonprofit ponds, and I always have been. Now, I choose to fish in for-profit ponds because those are the people serving on the nonprofit boards. I'm always trying new things. Put yourself out there. Don't be afraid to take the action that will differentiate you. The longer you are in business, the wiser you become about which events to attend.

Prioritize the Cultivation and Stewardship of Relationships

The cultivation and stewardship of relationships—professional and personal—has allowed me to get a lot of repeat business. I looked last year to see what my retention rate is, and it was ninety-five percent, meaning that the vast majority of those clients come back to me.

I usually do a one-hour consultation with every client; we talk about what they want to accomplish. One thing I want to know from them, "How do you want to be communicated with? In your ideal world, what would make this a successful partnership?" Maybe they've had a bad experience in the past. Email or phone? Daily updates or a hands-off approach? Maybe they want to be in the loop every step of the way, or maybe they only want to be bothered when I need something from them. Everyone is different.

Any time I finish a major project, I assess what didn't work and what could be done differently. What can I learn from these situations so it doesn't happen again? I'm open to seeing how we could be better. I send a handwritten thank you note to every client. I also ask them in person, "Is there anything we could have done better, that I could have done better, or that we could have done differently? Maybe something you were expecting?"

Growth occurs when you are striving to be better and do better all the time. I've worked with some tough people, but I still ask those questions. Even if you work with someone who is a real jackass, you should still ask—just take their feedback with a grain of salt.

Evaluate Constantly

My focus during my first year of consulting had been on building the business and getting clients. I had seven or eight clients a month, and it was all I could do to keep up. The work I did in my first year asking my clients the above questions allowed me to determine what steps to take next.

I realize now that when I first started consulting, I undervalued myself on some projects. In the beginning, I took business where I could get it—including those difficult clients and undesirable projects. When it came to expenses, I learned quickly that giving away 35 percent of my income was something I wasn't prepared for.

I became more skilled at the pieces I was missing. I had to work diligently to understand every aspect of the business, from the basics—tracking expenses – to QuickBooks to taxes; I wanted to know everything, just like I had as a CEO. I learned that I still had that CEO mentality. I worked with decision makers and gained the variety I craved, so I was never bored. Before starting my business, I had reached a place in my career where I was no longer learning anything new. Now, I was learning new skills and finding it energizing.

The second year of being in business was about seeing where I needed to spend my time and what could be delegated. Knowing my market and knowing my worth became critical. I had a moment when I realized I needed to raise my rates and start getting help in certain areas.

The third year was about looking at partnerships so I could provide a turnkey solution. How could I improve my product? I brought on five partners—female business owners I had worked with and trusted—and said, "We're going to sign non-competes, conflict-of-interest waivers, and agree to a percentage for referrals." I didn't want employees. I wanted women I could support and women who wanted to support me.

I realized I preferred having someone else work on grant writing. So now, when a client needs grant writing, I can say, "Awesome. I have someone for you." You need someone to run a special event? "Great. I have somebody for you." I didn't want to do marketing for my clients either, so I partnered with another consultant who does that. It was a way to have passive income and grow my network, and I was able to support other women to build their businesses.

Now I'm at a point where every day, I spend my time intentionally—what I do, where I go, who I partner with. I was wise enough to leverage my network and set things up in a way that if I get myself in a bind or something comes up, I know who I can refer work to; I know their quality. It requires top-notch communication and a shared vision, but if a client needs to hire somebody, our response is, "We have the *perfect* person for that." I continue to set measurable goals every year. I also reflect on the goals I accomplished because it is important to have a moment of pause. It's not always perfect, but I want to be able to look at how I've spent my time and know that I gave the business every single possible chance, leveraged every network, supported other women, and created something with everything I had. The passion is there, and I love doing it every day.

In addition to that pure passion, you need to be able to communicate your mission in a way that, (a) makes sense to people and (b) makes them want to either hire you or connect you with someone who needs your product or service. So, in the next chapter, we'll discuss another a major key to a building a successful business: ensuring that you have a well-crafted story.

Exercise: Evaluate and Identify Your Fear

Identify whatever fear is holding you back. Is it fear of failure, success, judgement, criticism or commitment? Something else?

Make a list of your top five fears in business and in your personal life. Arrange them in order of the influence they have over your life choices. Identifying those fears is the first step to overcoming them. You must understand the basis of what is holding you back before you can move forward.

TOP 5 FEARS

IN BUSINESS

1. _____
_____

2. _____
_____

3. _____
_____

4. _____
_____

5. _____
_____

PERSONAL

1. _____
_____

2. _____
_____

3. _____
_____

4. _____
_____

5. _____
_____

Chapter 8

Craft Your Story

"Follow your passion. It will lead to your purpose."

—OPRAH WINFREY

Everyone has a story. But not everyone is comfortable sharing it.

Crafting your story is vital to success. So is learning how to communicate it effectively, catering it to your niche and demonstrating how your unique set of circumstances made you the perfect person to do what you do. If you don't need help with your story, you may be able to skip this chapter. But if you are the kind of person who does not like talking about yourself, or you don't know what you should be sharing with people, I wrote this chapter specifically for you. It features a practical, step-by-step guide to writing out your story.

One of my clients referred me to a woman who we'll call Louise. She was the CEO of a healthy food delivery service and wanted to participate in a Pitch Day, an event put on by our local Chamber of Commerce for their Business Startup Scholars Program. She had an allotted time to pitch her business, discuss its strengths and weaknesses, and ask for support. If selected as a winner, she would be matched with a mentor, a coach, or a team to help her with a marketing plan to catapult her business.

The catch? Louise had never done any public speaking in her entire life.

I met with Louise and identified three main problems.

1. She didn't like to speak about her business in public.

2. She had no idea how to position herself.

3. She lacked confidence.

Louise was in her twenties, and while her business wasn't a nonprofit, I decided to take her on as a client because I have a soft place in my heart for seeing women succeed. I asked her what she wanted to get out of the experience other than to create a perfect pitch.

She said, "Well, I don't like to speak about my business in public."

"Well," I said, "that's going to be a problem because … well, because you run a business."

She told me her story. Louise was an unwed mother, about seven months pregnant at the time, when she was sitting at her kitchen counter thinking, *what am I going to do?* She was watching her father gain a lot of weight due to an unhealthy diet. His main complaint was that he was working a lot and didn't have time to take care of his health.

As she told me this story, she was nearly crying, especially when she talked about her father and the challenges in his health. She wanted to inspire him to get healthy. So, Louise came up with the idea to cater fit, healthy meals for the busy working professional. (She had a long-term plan to provide baby food and make it holistic for all different types of diets.)

Louise was only in the second year of business but had grown revenue from $139,000 to over $800,000 and was nowhere near prepared for such massive growth. In that same time, she went from roughly 0 to 36 employees. She had to get a bigger kitchen as she had needed more than her current 10,000 square foot facility. She started dealing with higher-volume shipping demands and needed different vans. Meanwhile, she was also a working mom and studying two nights a week to become a pastor. But she wasn't seasoned enough to pitch her business.

I was amazed. Her business had grown so quickly. How was she doing it? For somebody who had never managed her own business, she was doing as well as she could. She wanted to win Pitch Day because she was hoping to get someone to help her with an operational business plan, assist with the personal growth, and maybe manage the infrastructure of her business.

I asked her who she thought her biggest competitor was, and she didn't know. This was a problem because it meant she was unable to position herself when speaking to others. She needed to know who her competitors were, what they offered, and how she was different. Louise had staff members managing her website and marketing and felt she didn't really need to speak about her business. But she was going to have to *get* comfortable with speaking, so I thought I might as well prepare her for the Pitch Day while we were at it.

"How much time do we have?" I asked.

"Two weeks."

Two weeks. Okay....

We were going to have to focus on both crafting her story and communicating it effectively—and we had to move quickly. Even I didn't realize how difficult it would be. The following are the steps we used to make it happen.

Step 1: Write Out Your Story

We started with the basics. Her first homework assignment was to write down the story she had shared with me. I created a template of how we were going to lay out her pitch. If you have not done this for yourself, take the time to do it now. Here is the process:

1. **Why you started your business.** Include an overview of where you were in your life at the time. (For example, Louise wrote down the challenges of an unwed, pregnant mom and how she came up with her plan.)

2. **Business growth.** Include metrics such as growth in number of employees, revenue, and profits. (Louise also needed to include meals served per day. She didn't know a lot of the metrics, so that became part of the homework.)

3. **Share client success stories.** What is the problem you help people solve? What are the results? (In Louise's case, her father ended up losing forty pounds by using her service and became much healthier. She said, "It makes me feel good to know he'll live longer and can physically play with his grandson." An excellent testimonial, straight from the source.)

Step 2: Perfect Your Story

Even if you are not participating in a formal pitch event, you are pitching yourself or your business every time you open your mouth. Remember, you are the product.

Louise and I were meeting three times a week. We walked through the whole pitch step-by-step and worked nonstop. Two weeks was a short deadline even under ideal circumstances. We worked a long time at drafting her speech before I asked her to stand up and actually talk. You will need to do the same.

1. **Create a script.** Craft your story, and read it over and over again, refining it as you go. Cut out what doesn't work and add elements that will hit home with your target audience.

2. **Read, recite, repeat.** Practice reading your script out loud. Repeat it until it becomes second nature.

3. **Memorize it.** Get so comfortable with telling your story that you no longer need the script. If you have trouble with this or think you won't remember under pressure, develop "trigger points" within your script to help you remember the next phase.

The biggest challenge with Louise was not only getting her comfortable with telling her story, but getting her comfortable in public in general. I would see her at cocktail parties and networking events, and she was a bit awkward, but she had had this incredible growth in her business, and was trying to keep up with it. She had also recently been through a lawsuit. A company in the same state had a very similar name, and she had to fight for the name and the product. She had been through some pretty adult situations but not enough to develop the confidence she needed. I knew it would come in time, but would it come in two weeks? Either way, helping her tell her story was the first step.

Step 3: Tell Your Story and Do Not Forget to Ask for the Business

Louise lacked confidence. She kept getting lost in her words. By the time we took the script away, we had come up with some different signals I could use from the audience to help her remember, but she was still getting lost in the facts and figures.

1. **Take the script away.** No visual aids allowed! Memorize your script until you can say it in your sleep.

2. **Practice your trigger points.** And if it's an option, ask someone in the audience to provide a predetermined set of signals if you get lost.

3. **Identify the main point.** Connect with what really matters to your target customer.

Louise was struggling to stay confident about the process, partially because she didn't think people were going to be moved by her father's story. I felt that was a fair concern, but what was really missing for Louise was a connection to her customer's pain point.

I asked her how many people she knew who were struggling with their weight. How many people did she know who struggled with cooking healthy meals? This helped her get clarity on her target customer (a single mom or a busy professional). Once she was on stage, I told her to ask, "How many of you are so pressed for time that you have to get dinner at a fast food drive-through?" Then I told her to pause to let people raise their hands.

I soon realized we had so little time that I didn't think winning Pitch Day was a realistic expectation. I told her no matter the outcome, she should be proud for all the hard work she had done. And I say the same to you. Regardless of whether a specific prize is at stake, you are still going to need to be the face of your company. Consider going into Toastmasters or investing in personal coaching to get comfortable speaking in public or one on one.

Step 4: Wow the Crowd

told Louise to find out if she could bring food to the event. This was a golden opportunity to have the judges and the audience taste her product. I asked what samples she could serve that were simple to make, transportable, and easy to eat. She decided on a specialty sample that would work.

1. **Set yourself apart**. Identify something totally unique about what you offer, and use it to differentiate yourself from the crowd.

2. **Provide samples**. If you run a product-based business, bring samples to share. If you run a service-based business, think about how you can have your customers experience your product. (For example, offer them a coupon for a twenty-minute session, a free webinar, or an eBook.)

As it turned out, I wasn't allowed to attend Pitch Day, so I couldn't provide the signals we had decided on. It would all be on Louise. She taped the event, and I watched later. She had food brought in, like we had discussed, and everybody was thrilled because they were starving. I watched the footage, thinking, *I knew it. You bring food, and you will have fans.*

She didn't always make eye contact. There were some places where she was nervous, but she did deliver 90 percent of the content. At the end, she made her ask – based on my story, the growth I am experiencing in my business, do you see any reason why I am not the next Start-Up Scholar? And she paused to wait for a response. I was proud of her. Given the timelines, she had done a phenomenal job and remembered what I always tell fund raisers – if you do not ask, you do not get.

Louise won the scholarship, and the success of her pitch meant she could continue with ongoing coaching. She successfully implemented her operational, discontinued working the van shipping system herself, and outsourced shipping. Her attention quickly shifted to getting a bigger kitchen. A year later, her business was in the Tampa International Airport. She not only has a business where they deliver healthy food directly to your house; she is now providing healthy options at the airport to those who travel.

If you see any of yourself in Louise and dislike speaking in front of crowds, sharing your story, or networking of any kind—and especially if *you* are your business—give yourself the gift of walking through the preceding steps and the additional suggestions at the end of this chapter. Then you can craft a pitch for your networking events, whether it be a social event, a formal business event, or in the grocery store. You would be surprised how much confidence you gain by knowing what you are going to say when people ask. And they will ask!

When you know your story, and implement a few practical steps to develop that story to maximum effectiveness, you can truly communicate what it is you do and how you help people.

Exercise: Perfecting Your Story

Ask Yourself:
   a. What do you want your story/elevator speech/ sales pitch to do for you?
   b. Are there any other outcomes you would like to get out of the ask?

Do Your Research

    a. Who are your top three competitors?

    b. What do they offer?

    c. What distinguishes you?

    d. Know your numbers and outcomes.

Chapter 9

Find a Mentor

"To be successful, you must get results. To be significant, you must help others get results."

—MACK STORY

Mentorship opportunities are invaluable resources for young women. Unfortunately, this was an area that was tragically underserved until recent years. There were many times in college, for instance, when I felt like the odd woman out. I didn't personally know *anyone* who was as driven to excel or focused on achieving big things after they graduated as I was. I didn't have friends with the ambition to travel the world. I always struggled to find people to talk to who were goal-setting like me. In many ways, it was a lonely road.

It wasn't until I entered the for-profit sector that I connected with like-minded people from whom I could learn. That's what a mentor is: a like-minded person within your chosen field, or someone who possesses shared values, who is more experienced and further along in their journey.

My advice is to find a good mentor or two and get counsel. Early on, I had a lot of mentors who I listened to and trusted implicitly. A lot of them were men because female mentors were difficult to find at the time, but fortunately, I always seemed to get good guidance from them. If you're a people pleaser or you've always taken your parents' advice, you might be more likely to do as your mentor tells you without question. However, I suggest you always take the advice of a mentor—or anyone, for that matter—with a grain of salt.

The Value of a Good Mentor

I have always had male mentors and only recently female mentors. The reason for this is two-fold. First, the female leaders in my community when I was rising through the ranks provided limited access to other females. Second, women in leadership roles were hesitant to "pay it forward," worried about competition or feeling that others should experience the same difficulty they may have encountered, like a rite of passage.

In the museum world, my mentor was Tom Gessler. I met him when I was interning at the Museum of Fine Arts in St. Pete. He was a father figure. He moved me in and out of all of my apartments and helped line up a job when I came out of Florida State University, where I worked for a few months. He was the one who encouraged me to take the job in Vero Beach to increase my level of responsibility, and when I was leaving to get my master's, he helped find me the *Titanic* opportunity. He was even at my wedding. He retired in 2015 after working in the same museum for forty-five years. Tom gave me great guidance and helped me to see what was possible in that world.

I found that my male mentors focused on practicality. Men tend to think very linearly and would often tell me exactly what I should do. Later, when I had female mentors, the guidance was very different. It was geared more around emotional intelligence.

Once I started transitioning into fundraising, I was mentored by Lloyd Horton from All Children's Hospital and a woman named Nina Berkheiser. I was just getting started in fundraising and needed mentoring about many of the mechanics: Where do I start? What do I need to learn about ethics? What do I need to learn about how to build a proper development program? Nina was excellent at laying the foundation and giving me honest feedback.

When I wanted to go into the CEO role, I struggled to find a mentor, and I definitely could have used one with the challenges I was facing. But there just weren't many women in similar positions available or accessible in the area. Nina would still help me with fundraising and business plans, but there really weren't any women running art museums.

This was the only time in my professional life when I didn't have a mentor. I didn't have anybody to lean on professionally. I had a very good friend who worked with me as CFO, but I didn't have anybody willing to work with me as a mentor. It was difficult to even find a male mentor, I think because of my age.

Having good mentors is critical to success. I recommend a local mentor, as there is accessibility. Meeting in person, face-to-face, really matters. Part of the mentor-mentee relationship is about hearing stories or advice from a different perspective, which in turn allows you to think more introspectively. Some of it is about having someone you can lean on when you've had a bad day or somebody's bruised your ego.

Mentors aren't supposed to be daisies and sunshine all the time. Their job is to challenge you. Receiving advice from them forces you to know yourself and assess whether or not you should take their advice. Leadership gets developed by learning the appropriate way to react and take action under different circumstances. No matter what sort of mentor relationship you have, my advice is to listen to what they have to say based on their experiences.

It is best to have more than one mentor, but the first step is to make sure your mentor has a vested interest in your success and knows your vision and goals. The following is a checklist/game plan for making big decisions, including finding a good mentor.

How to Make Big Decisions

1. Plan Your Course

- Set a goal—have a vision for your life and career.

- Make a list of pros/cons.

- Sit with a decision for a while.

2. Ask Questions

- How am I going to ultimately benefit from this?

- How is this going to add value to my life?

- What is my endgame?

3. Follow Your Gut

- When pros/cons lists fail, trust your instincts.

- Happiness and fulfillment always trump practicality and obligation.

- Remember: What's right for someone else may not be right for you.

4. Get Counsel from Mentors

- Listen to mentors' advice, but never follow it blindly.

- Ask yourself: Does my mentor have *my* best interests at heart?

- When in doubt, get a second opinion.

Tips for a Successful Mentor/Mentee Relationship

The following is a list of helpful suggestions to help facilitate a "meaningful relationship" with your mentor. These suggestions are for mentees and mentors alike and are designed to ensure that your mentoring experience is fulfilling and beneficial for all involved. Utilize these tips for a more effective and productive relationship.

CONVERSATION STARTERS FOR YOUR UPCOMING MEETING

Mentee: Begin by Asking Your Mentor....

- Who inspired you to be a leader?

- What was the career path that led you to your current position?

- What challenges have you faced in your career?

- What lessons have you learned from your successes and failures?

- What do you do for your own growth and development?

Mentor: Begin by Asking Your Mentee....

- What makes you, you?

- What values drive your actions?

- What life experiences have influenced you the most?

- What is your strongest attribute?

- What unique skills and competencies do you possess?

ONCE A CONNECTION IS MADE, GET TOGETHER RIGHT AWAY

Schedule your first meeting as soon as you can, to help establish momentum. It is too easy to let other priorities get in the way unless you commit to making the most of this opportunity. In-person meetings are the best way to get to know one another, but video calls can also work well.

Wait to bring up sensitive topics and tough questions until after you have built trust. You're bound to get better advice that way—and to receive more quality feedback, versus a "quick fix."

Draft a mentoring plan. This doesn't have to be anything formal. A plan that is clear and concise often works best.

Simply summarize what you want to accomplish together so you're both on the same page.

Clarify expectations. How do you want your relationship to work? What type of support do you need? Decide when you'll meet and if you want a specific agenda each time. How do you want to handle communications? Bring up confidentiality, feedback preferences, and other topics that are crucial to you.

STAY CONNECTED

Stay on track. Check in at least monthly, sometimes weekly during the beginning or when key challenges or opportunities arise. Be proactive. This is all about your future. Address small problems before they become challenging. Face-to-face meetings, Skype calls, conference calls, and email are among the many ways you can stay in touch.

Manage expectations. Check in to see how you're progressing; are you making real progress toward your goals? Revisit your mentoring plan. Do you need to shift gears based on what you've learned with your mentor? Pose open-ended questions to one another to probe deeper.

Inquire about the relationship. Is it working for both of you? Keep in mind that your mentor is volunteering their time to support you and to help you reach your goals. It's a great time to say thank you. Like any relationship, problems may occur. Take care to keep perspective. Staying positive and having a sense of humor often helps.

RENEW OR MOVE AHEAD

Mentoring relationships typically last a year or more. It's up to both of you to consider renewing your relationship.

When to renew. If you have a good relationship and are still learning, you may want to renew and update your mentoring plan while you're at it.

When to move ahead. If you've achieved most of your goals, that's the ideal time to say thanks and move on. On the other hand, maybe you haven't made as much progress as you expected or the relationship isn't working for a variety of other reasons (e.g., a shift in goals, unclear goals, lack of commitment, unrealistic expectations, etc.). Think about what worked and what didn't. That way, you can learn and be better prepared for your next mentoring relationship.

Again—say thanks! Celebrate a little. If you achieved a great deal, celebrate all the more. What if things didn't go as planned? Remember that no relationship is all smooth sailing. We're all complex. Remember that you both made an investment, and reaching goals isn't easy.

Consulting Your Mentor for Advice

Mentors are there to give you advice, but that doesn't mean you have to take it. Regardless of what you decide when you consult your mentor, you are sure to

155

learn something. Absorb the different viewpoints and then ultimately decide what is right for you.

Fundraising was a male-dominated field back in the early 2000s. But that trend has shifted since then. According to the Association of Fundraising Professionals, it is now female-dominated, with 80 percent of fundraising professionals being women. Across various fields and in many industries, young women have more opportunity now than ever. But make no mistake, there are still major challenges, obstacles, and detractors that stand in our way. Women also have more opportunity now to find mentors who are willing to work with them. Competition does still exist within fields of expertise, but the enormous importance of mentoring has shifted. More women are in positions where they are able to serve as mentors and are willing to help.

CASE STUDY: The Benefits of Mentoring

Since 2008, I have had the privilege of mentoring a woman who is a bit older than me. We will call her Olivia. Olivia came to me for assistance in increasing her fundraising skills within nonprofit. I felt both honored to be asked and a responsibility to pay it forward.

I had worked with Olivia over the course of six years at two separate organizations. She was part of a development team and managed volunteers at the time. She liked what she did but wanted to be doing more and making a bit more money.

I knew that if she really wanted to do more, we needed to work on her professional development plan. She needed to start getting that skill set and increasing her value. She loved the volunteer division because it made her feel warm and fuzzy, but she now had to start generating revenue. We worked on defining what that would look like, where she should be spending her time, and how to cultivate prospects. Her goal was to become a certified fundraising executive (CFRE). We reorganized her job and ultimately moved her into a special events role so she could still work with volunteers while developing a portfolio of donors.

When I later moved on to a different organization and had to reassemble a team, I hired Olivia. I continued to give her more responsibility and eventually recruited her into the development director role, managing that department.

Her perpetual problem was that she "didn't have enough time." So, I worked with her on her time management plans. Soon, the problem became clear: She was doing everything herself. Olivia was frequently taking it upon herself to fulfill duties that could easily be delegated. She said she did not have enough time, yet she would stay up until all hours of the night stuffing baskets for a special event. She was good at everything she did, but she was going to burn herself out. She had to get better at delegating and allocating tasks to other people, and she had to be comfortable with giving up control.

Since *time* was her Achilles heel, I had her make a time management chart (see Chapter 5) to study how she was spending her day. I wanted her to escape the mindset of having to do everything herself because it had to be done a certain way.

I connected Olivia with different professional development groups and guided her to the point where she could serve on boards herself, which would also help her down her career path. After seven years, when I left to start my own business, she was devastated. Everywhere she went in a professional capacity, she would call me up and say, "They're not like you." It was a nice compliment to hear that she missed working with me, but I gently reminded her that she would have to figure out how to work with other people and discover *their* expectations.

She ultimately became the CEO of a nonprofit foundation.

In her first year, she has stabilized the organization by creating a strategic plan, authentically engaged the volunteers, and increased the profile of the organization. I was fortunate to be able to help her with many of these goals as an executive coach and consultant. A year later, the board was pleased as punch with her.

Only once did they ever asked me, "How do you know her?"

"Well, we worked together," I say. We never say she's a protégé or that I'm her mentor. The goal is for *her* to shine, for her to see what her potential is.

Olivia is one of my best success stories. Over the years, I have mentored her on issues that have evolved as her career has advanced: fundraising, ethics, management, volunteerism, and executive leadership. I have watched her blossom into a more confident, capable, and connected woman. In addition, I have encouraged her and paved the way for her to serve the community through boards such as the Association of Fundraising Professionals.

Eight years ago, Olivia was managing volunteers. I'm not downplaying the importance of that work, but if she hadn't decided to try for something bigger, just look at all the skills that would have gone unrealized! Look at all the positive change that has been manifested thanks to her ambition to move up. She also has confidence in herself, now.

We need more women like Olivia, and I know she will help to develop the next generation of female leaders. What I did not count on was what she has provided me, teaching me how to be a more vulnerable, softer, and gentler soul.

Pay It Forward

Recently, I was on the syndicated lifestyle show *Daytime* to talk about mentoring and was asked the question, "What is the greatest benefit of mentoring?" The answer is simple: personal growth. The difference in personal growth between women with mentors vs. those without is striking.

The lack of a reliable system for women to participate in mentor-mentee relationships is something I feel needs to be corrected. It is an evolving progress that is very important to the professional development of Millennial women.

I am happy to say that I am actively participating in groups who seek to overcome this issue. As I will discuss in further detail in Chapter 12, I have been involved in launching mentoring programs for college and entrepreneurial women.

In life, you will have many mentors, some for a short time, some for a long time, and all for different purposes. But I believe a true mentor helps you grow personally first, so that the lessons can permeate into your professional life, ultimately building your true character.

Chapter 10

Grow Your Reputation Wisely – It's All You Have

"To build trust, a leader must exemplify competence, connection, and character."

—JOHN C. MAXWELL

D uring my first year in business, I taught a class on change management at a nonprofit leadership center called Leading Change. It was based on the book *Leading Change* by John P. Kotter. We took a business principle and applied it to the nonprofit world.

The class was appropriate for CEOs who were put in an environment to push or implement some type of change like strategic planning. Maybe they were doing a capital campaign, or there was some shift in the organization. Of course, every CEO in the class had different reasons why they were there.

CASE STUDY: Leading Change

A young man in the course was a first-time CEO. For the sake of the story, let's call him Rob. Rob had come up through the fundraising ranks with other organizations and was getting ready to start working at a large nonprofit.

Rob wanted to increase revenue at the company. He felt there were problems among the staff, and one of the first areas we talked about was what he needed to do to make that happen. Number one, he needed to create a sense of urgency. How do you do that among your staff? How do you communicate that there is going to be change? How do you make it clear that if we don't start to do this now, here's what the detriment will look like?

The following are the steps I walked him through.

Step One: Form a powerful coalition. How do you do that? Depending on the environment, that could mean your board, volunteers, or your leadership team. Who are you going to get to buy into the vision and help you push this along?

Step Two: Create a vision. It's one thing to have a vision, but if you turn around and nobody's following you, the vision clearly isn't shared. How do you get your vision to come across clearly? You have to continue to communicate at every meeting, at every turn, so that the stakeholders understand what you're trying to accomplish.

Step Three: Remove obstacles. Obstacles could be human capital. They could be some of the job descriptions—people simply not doing things because they don't feel it's "their job." How do you remove the barriers that exist to be successful and implement change?

Step Four: Create a short-term win. If the changes are long-term, the staff needs benchmarks; they need to see some success. The progress needs to be visible to them in the form of short-term wins so they can continue to be led along.

Step Five: Build on the change. That means celebrating together, continuing to set goals together, and keeping ideas fresh by having people onboard who bring in ideas and solutions, versus bringing in problems.

We talked about all of these steps as part of the course, but Rob was struggling with a lot of the changes he was attempting to implement. He asked me to come and perform an assessment of his fundraising team. He had come up through the fundraising ranks and was not programmatic in nature. He felt like he had a lot of different irons in the fire. While he did have a gut feeling about what was wrong and what wasn't, he wanted my assessment to either validate his thoughts or help open him up to something new and fresh.

I spent three months in his organization doing a development assessment. I covered the current team, their skill sets, the job descriptions, how they were doing in revenue production, their marketing efforts—everything within that spectrum. My report outlined what was going right and what Rob might want to consider updating or changing.

After that, Rob came to me frequently, and I become more involved with his organization. We worked well together, he believed in the product, and my assistance helped them move the needle as he began implementing some of the suggestions from my assessment.

CASE STUDY: Leading Chaos

Rob had been the CEO of this organization for three years when he approached me again with a request. One of his employees on the development team was leaving on maternity leave. He was not sure whether she would be coming back. Since I knew his team so well, he asked if I would be able to onboard in the interim and keep the plate spinning until her return. I said, "Sure." It would be a couple of hours a week. The team liked me and trusted me, and I knew their mission and business model.

About a month before I came on board, the individual who was leaving decided for sure that she wasn't going to come back. The dynamics changed, but I agreed to stick with the contract and help out. It would give Rob time to make an assessment and determine whether he wanted to use me to hire somebody, and he didn't need to be under pressure trying to find someone.

Within my first month in that role, I watched three people either quit or get fired. I started paying attention to the types of people who were being let go. Many of them were female and either single, single mothers, or pregnant.

I started listening to their stories. I learned that the perception around the office was that you were expected to be accessible and available at all hours, which made these women feel guilty. I knew of at least two women on antidepressants and anxiety medication thanks to this implied obligation to always be on-call.

Then I began watching Rob's behaviors—what he said in the hallways and the way he would speak to his employees. From an HR standpoint, he had no discretion. He was arrogant. He was sarcastic and demeaning in staff meetings, and was constantly putting staff members down. At the end of the day, he was just a bully. It was strange. I had never gotten that impression from him before. I thought, *what happened to this guy?*

In typical first-year CEO fashion, Rob wanted everybody to work as he did: around the clock. He wasn't married and didn't have kids. He was your typical Type A, workaholic, go-getter personality, and he expected all of his employees to be the same. He had succeeded in creating a sense of urgency in his organization, but the way he went about it was causing problems. He wasn't a motivator at all. In fact, he was actively de-motivating them.

As for the bullying and the sarcasm, that is classic first-time leader behavior. It's a way of trying to appear more like a peer than a leader. Making offhand, flippant comments to appear relaxed and easy-going. He was trying to ingratiate himself with the staff through casual banter, but the reality was that no one was going to banter back with him because what he said wasn't casual. It was cutting.

After two *more* people left, I wondered if I could make a difference if I sat down with him about the changes and behvaiors I had been observing.

I went into Rob's office one day, and we started talking about somebody who had just left. He said, "Well, they didn't really fit in with the culture, anyway."

"She was here for five years," I said. "How did she *stop* fitting in with the culture?" He started nitpicking things about this person, and I said, "Is it possible that maybe there is something else going on? Something in the way that you're dealing with the staff that's the problem? Because a lot of people have left in the past six months."

He dismissed this, saying all those people just weren't a "good fit."

"Okay," I said. "Why?"

"I don't know," he said. "I think I get along with pretty much everybody."

I finally said, "You know, Rob, I'm going to put myself out there and tell you this. I have to tell you, a lot of people here think you're a bully. Many of them think you're sarcastic. As a result, there are a lot of people here who are unhappy. I'm sharing this with you because I'd like to introduce you to somebody, so you can get a mentor as a first-time CEO, if you're open to it." I knew the perfect person. He was another client I had met the same way—another male who had his share of bumps and bruises.

Unfortunately, it became very clear that Rob was not going to respond to me. He had no interest. He felt like everybody else was the issue.

The next day, *another* person quit. She called me and told me about it. She went out on a limb and told him the truth. She told him, "I'm quitting because I'm on antianxiety medication because of this job," and she brought up three or four specific examples of ways he had spoken to her that made her uncomfortable.

His response: "I don't recall that."

Just *one day* before, I'd attempted to help him course-correct. I had opened up, shown a little bit of vulnerability, shared what was happening in his organization, and told him how I could help. And a day later, this happens.

And he still didn't take the bait.

When Good People Get Lost in Business

This whole situation was upsetting to me. This person simply could not see that *he* was the common denominator, and he was not even open to trying to understand what was happening. It is a perfect example of how people sometimes get into a position where they lose perspective—they lose *themselves* in business.

Rob needed a mentor, but was not open to it, despite the fact that a mentor could have potentially helped him in huge ways personally and professionally. He wasn't even listening to employees who were telling him point-blank exactly what he was doing wrong, even as they were leaving. He just wasn't going to listen to anybody. It made me sad. I knew he was just trying to prove himself, but he got lost along the way.

This was also hard because I had such a good relationship with Rob and had done so much with organization. He had changed to the point that I wondered if he even had the maturity to keep things in this professional context anymore.

Unfortunately, and predictably, Rob ended up laying off over 5 individuals in 7 months and over 4 people resigned within the year. Many were people who had been at the organization for fifteen or twenty years and just couldn't do it anymore.

Not only is this a testimony to the kinds of challenges women and men end up having to navigate in the business world, but it's also a cautionary tale about the pitfalls of foolish pride as a leader. It's hard to watch when somebody at the helm of an organization is too prideful to seek out a mentor. When the leader is not open to growing, the organization suffers. They have high staff turnover, which looks bad in the community and makes it difficult to hire. At the end of the day, it is the board's responsibility to hire and fire that CEO, but the last time I checked, the board wasn't paying attention or fulfilling their role. It was painful to watch, knowing that things could have been so much different with a little humility.

I look back, and I want to tell Rob, "We trained in the rules of Leading Change. But you're not leading change. You're leading chaos."

Chapter 11

Avoid the Detractors

*"If you believe in it, it's important to you.
It's a fire that cannot be put out."*

—Anonymous

There will always be somebody who either doesn't believe in you or discourages you from trying to pursue your goals. Additionally, there will be things and events that get in the way of your goals. You will inevitably encounter disheartening circumstances and setbacks. I call these people and events "detractors."

When I look back, it's amazing to realize that *every* major event in my life could have easily been derailed by any number of detractors. With every risk I've ever taken, there has always been a detractor, be it a mental or physical health issue, a naysayer, or a financial impediment.

Mentally preparing for the *Titanic* expedition and then being out at sea, without any outside support from family and friends, was a real test. When I took the risk to become CEO, I had no clue of the stamina and brainpower required to simultaneously balance running an organization, raising a three-year-old, and being pregnant. Life circumstances can become major detractors. Unfortunately, many people don't see them at the time.

Sometimes, detractors come from unlikely places. I have found many detractors in the form of people, even mentors. When I started my business, my mentor asked me why I wanted that business model. She said, "Nobody wants to do that stuff." That was crushing. I share that story frequently to demonstrate that you shouldn't always listen to mentors. My response was, "Because nobody is offering it, and that is what is needed." Fortunately, I didn't let it derail me. I kept moving forward.

The biggest detractor for me when I started my business was other people's doubt in my abilities and their negative comments. These become all the more potent when they come from someone close to you.

The Most Devastating Detractors

I remember when I told my husband I was leaving my job. His response was, "You're doing *what*? What are you going to do for money?" It was not, "I support you," or,

"That's exciting." It was a devil's advocacy scenario. I had never felt so unsupported in my life.

Two days later, he took $50,000 out of our savings account, moved it into cash, and went to our financial advisor. I was so offended because it made me feel like he didn't think I was going to be successful. It felt like he didn't believe in me. Of course, that is not at all what he meant. He thought it would show me he *did* believe in me. He felt bad for what he had said, but I thought, *you are just digging a hole. I'll show you.*

I never touched that money. After about a year and a half in business, when we received our tax returns, for the first time in seventeen years, I had the bulk of the refund. That made me feel really good. I had not missed a beat financially. I looked at him and said, "I think you can put the money back now."

I have worked with men who felt threatened because of my strong personality, ambition, and decisiveness. They were easier to ignore, but it's harder to brush off your mentors, your spouse, and anyone in your trusted circle. For example, many women are held back because they don't deal with an issue they had with a parent, and it affects them their entire lives. Detractors are particularly powerful when they come from the people closest to you.

It gets complicated with spouses. If you have a spouse or significant other who is unhappy in their work life while you are thriving, that can also be a detractor. It makes you worry; you become hesitant to let your light shine too bright. Many women suffer from that mindset, and it is absolutely crippling to their ability to thrive. You have to tell yourself, "That is not my problem!"

It is not your responsibility to hold yourself back for someone else's benefit. It's not that I don't have empathy, but I do believe that many women I've met cannot move forward because they are afraid to outshine their husband or to avoid conflict within the relationship.

I have since learned that my husband is more *reactive* in certain situations, and he thinks about it later. Still, at the time, those words and thoughts and feelings could have been major detractors from me doing what I felt I needed to do. Those things stick with you. Be wary of people in your life who may not support you—even if they are well-meaning. And ignore them and trust your gut.

Exercise: Expose Your Detractors

1. **Identify.** Write a list of all the things that are detractors for you—these could be people, things, events, or places that will pull you off-purpose and bring all your forward progress to a grinding halt.

2. **Plan.** What is your plan of action for when somebody is not supportive? What will you do/say?

3. **Rely.** Who are the people who you can trust and rely on? The people who are truly in your corner?

Tuning Out the Noise

The most important thing to learn is how to tune out the "noise" and not let detractors deter you from paving your own way and carrying on, even when things get hard. I've made it my mission to address all the things that were detractors for me—things that could have easily obstructed my ability to jump the queue.

To be clear, I'm fine with constructive criticism and advice, but when someone tells me I can't do something, it makes me want it even more. It also reminds me to pay closer attention the next time.

It seems like people—men in particular—have been trying to talk me out of jumping the queue my whole life. In the case of my father, his "advice" always had a hidden motive. He didn't want me to go to school in Boston because, "You'll freeze your ass off up there." When I wanted to study abroad, he said, "You don't want to go to another country. Why would you want to leave the USA?" I soon realized that he was giving me advice that had nothing to do with *me* or what *I* wanted. It was his way of maintaining control. He wanted me to stay. He wanted me to not want to do these things.

As a result of my father's attempts to control me, I tend to notice when others make similarly limiting comments. It's always in the *way* they say it. It's not that they don't believe you. It's not even constructive criticism. It's usually more leading. Things like, "You don't want to do that, do

175

you?" Or, "Do you really think that's a good idea?" Or, "That sounds very ambitious, but are you sure it's a good fit for *you*?"

Because of my father, I have always been able to see right through these "questions" and expose this behavior as an attempt at control. Even when I ask friends and female mentors for honest feedback, I still sometimes wonder if what they are saying is to help me or to keep me where I am. *Do they want me to be successful?*

How to Ignore the Naysayers

Chances are, there will be naysayers with every risk you ever take. If somebody is unsupportive, how do you pull yourself up from that? When I was young, I thought they were trying to warn me. I thought they were being a friend. My advice for millennial women is:

Have a strong belief in yourself. Develop a high level of confidence because there will be times in your life when *you* are the only one believing in you. When I was starting my consulting business, I kept a positive mindset and did not let the opinions, judgments and fears of others interfere with my deep certainty that I would be successful. I didn't let fears of money or replacing my income get in my way. I trusted in myself and my abilities.

Be open to opportunities. No one's forcing you to stay in your chosen lane. Consider how you could transfer your skills. Some really amazing things happen when you're not as rigid about how you apply the skills you learned in your field of study.

Go with your gut. People in their twenties and thirties who have gone to school for "x" number of years often feel obligated to get a job in their field of study. They beat themselves up if they can't get a job, or they try to force themselves to fit in somewhere they hate. Let go of what you *think* you want to do—or what you think you *should* do.

My mom used to tell me to make a list of the pros and the cons. I still find myself doing that, but at the end of the day, if I'm still chewing on something, a pros and cons list might not cut it. If it's something I still want three days later, I just do it. If I had relied solely on pros and cons lists, I might never have gone over to the for-profit sector in the first place.

Of course, going with your gut isn't easy. A lot of times, you have to work for it. I'll give you an example. Back when my work was a CEO, I felt it would be beneficial to become a certified fundraising executive (CFRE). I was still doing fundraising all the time, and felt that becoming certified would legitimize the level of expertise I had, and it was something I wanted. My mentor at the time discouraged me from pursuing this. Cue the detractor control questions: "Are you really fundraising that much? Do you *really* need to be certified in that, now that you're in more of an administrative role?" I understand now that my mentor was trying to get me to think hard about this goal and determine whether it was a good fit for my new path, but it was difficult to hear. It never feels good to present an idea to someone whose opinion you respect, only to be dismissed.

To add insult to injury, I didn't pass the test the first time. I missed it by one point. I had never not passed a test in my life. I didn't pass it the second time I tried, either. I felt like John F. Kennedy Jr., who famously failed the bar exam twice and vowed that if he kept failing, he'd keep taking it until he passed, even if it meant trying until he was ninety-five.

The first time, I had studied on my own. The second time, I had tried to find a study group. The third time, I found a woman who was teaching a two-day course who was the former director of CFRE and had helped write the test questions. The third time was the charm, and I became a certified fundraising executive. When I look back on what was the defining moment for me, it was how I took the test. I had come to a point where I had the "practical experience" and was applying it to the questions and answer process. This was not how the test was structured. Questions were created with "distractors" and were directly from textbooks. I had to learn how to deconstruct the question and yes, study. Again.

I tend to be harder on the mentor who discouraged me from becoming a CFRE than I am on other detractors, even though I know it wasn't anything personal. To this day, I continue to re-certify and maintain this important credential. It was a lesson on not giving up and knowing that if you truly want something bad enough, you will find a way. You do not allow detractors, ego, or your fear of humiliation to get in the way.

Expose your detractors for what they are. Refuse to let them derail your progress. And most of all, be on the lookout for those leading questions so often directed at young women to try to rein in their ambitions. The control they insultingly attempt to impose can change the course of a young woman's life.

The harsh reality is that many people, sometimes even your friends and family, don't want you to shine that bright. The people who have your best interests at heart are those who will provide constructive criticism and feedback but will then tell you to go for it.

You really want it? Then go for it.

Chapter 12

Leave a Legacy
– Service Above Self

"Giving is the highest level of living."

—JOHN MAXWELL

I n my twenties, I had served on boards because it would benefit my career. When I hit my thirties, I was more intentional. It became more about giving back and serving beyond self. For me, that meant the YMCA.

The YMCA was an escape from the adversity in my home life. When my parents divorced, my father pulled a lot of the child support away from my mom. That meant we qualified as scholarship recipients at the YMCA, so it was where we went on the weekends. It was where we learned how to swim. At the Y, you were just a normal kid. You were around other kids, having fun, and nobody really knew your home situation.

As an adult, I remember thinking, *If I am ever able to do something to give back, the first thing has to be the Y.* So, I started serving there and used my fundraising experience to help bring in money so that children could benefit from those same services I had received when I was a child, including helping with small grants. I know what a financial challenge it is for these kids to go to summer camp, I've been there.

For a few years, I served on the board. Eventually, they asked me to be president of the board. The Y is largely a male-dominated organization—not surprising given that YMCA stands for Young Men's Christian Association. In fact, I was only the second female president of the board.

I'll never forget speaking to the staff about the annual fundraising campaign. There were around 150 staff present. I talked about discovering your *why*—the reason you do what you do. I told my story about how I had been coming to this YMCA since I was eight years old. How I had been a scholarship kid. How people who had been here when I was a child were now coaching my children. Never in a million years would I have thought that the same eight-year-old who was sent to the Y during a difficult time in her life to learn to swim would someday serve as the president of its board. I told them that while I served as president, I would be here to tell my story to help raise money, construct a new building, and serve the Y.

Later a woman who worked at the Y approached me, in an exercise class, to let me know that my story had really touched her. Up until this point, everyone who had served as president was just résumé-building—the same way I used to think of serving on boards. It was the first time I realized that I could have such a big impact outside of just giving dollars and providing leadership.

This is what it's really about, I realized. *Serving above self, doing something I'm passionate about.*

I was so thankful for everything the Y had given me. Now, it was truly gratifying that I was able to return the favor. I served on that board for eight years.

Give Back and Pay It Forward

Think back to your most impactful life moments. Is there a person, community, or an organization that made a real difference to you? This is a great way to start learning what you are passionate about and how to give back.

Money can be regained if it's lost, but time is a different story. If you are going to do anything—take a job, volunteer, start a business, run an organization—it had better be something you're passionate about, because that's where you're spending your time outside of your family and your personal life.

Serve with an attitude of gratitude, and remember, it's not about you!

Service above self is all about paying it forward. Not everybody is equipped to sit on a board or be a president, but everyone can do something. Just volunteering, doing what you can, and using your passion to help people find theirs will make a difference.

The Power of Mentoring Programs

When I hit forty and started my business, my goals and ambitions started to change in big ways.

I wanted to focus on leaving a legacy, and that theme prevailed in every purposeful thing that I did. This is the message I want to leave you with in this final chapter.

A few years ago, I interviewed the woman who was running a program at the University of South Florida called Women's Leadership and Philanthropy. She told me about a "fledgling" mentoring program that was in development. "Why is it *fledgling*?" I asked.

"Well, everybody wants to do mentoring at the business school," she said, "but we are struggling to get young women in other academic areas the mentors they need."

"But you have a membership base of 250 incredible women," I said. "I don't understand why they can't line up."

I've always been a big believer in mentoring, and it concerned me that young women who were seeking guidance would have trouble finding it. Like so many things, it started by identifying a need. Before I knew it, I had signed up to come in as mentoring chair and had created a mentoring program.

In typical fashion, we were given only four areas where the school thought a mentoring program might be useful. The college of business was not one of them. *I thought, Really? Just four areas of study?* No college of business. No engineering. None of the traditionally male-dominated majors. Yet again, women are being relegated to the lesser sciences.

One of the areas we *were* given was athletics. Many female athletes, alarmingly, did not have plans in place for any sort of professional careers and had done absolutely nothing to prepare themselves for the real world. They didn't know how to interview. They didn't know how to present themselves outside of the realm of athletics. They were, in general, unprepared for life. This was an "ah ha" moment for me as I realized that there were women groups outside of the mainstream circles that needed guidance as well.

Our goal was to provide scholarships to young women who could not afford school, but I thought we needed to take it a step further and align them with a mentor, so we created a system that involved matching our members and benefactors with these young women so that they would be connected with mentors beyond just the financial need. As a result, the program became incredibly powerful, creating long-lasting relationships between young women and mentors who can now help them navigate real-world challenges.

That sort of thing never existed when I was growing up. It would have been so helpful. But now, it's coming together. Women helping women. Women coming from a place of abundance and not scarcity. Collaboration instead of competition. My second year, I served on the scholarship committee. Our goal was to make education accessible. I was given the opportunity to review 130 to 150 applications of women who were just like me. These weren't big scholarships, but they were for women who needed money and wanted to go into engineering or business or other fields. Many were the first in the family to go to college.

That mentoring program really set the path for me. I was proud of what we were doing at USF, but I couldn't accomplish everything I wanted to do in that environment. I thought, *wouldn't it be cool if we had a mentoring program for female entrepreneurs or women who were at later points in their career and maybe wanted to have a second act?*

Getting to them young during the college career was one thing. It's a different story for older women. The biggest challenge that women have in their thirties is that they are having children, getting married, *and* building their careers. Maybe they work a demanding job and just don't have time. This sort of thing, a mentoring program, didn't exist for when I was rising through the ranks. I was sure there were professionals out there who could benefit from this kind of program, so I sought out the founder of the largest networking group for women, Working Women of Tampa Bay, Jessica Rivelli. Together we created the Meaningful Mentoring program.

We had 110 applicants the first year. Many of these women were interested in making a career move in business. Some needed a mentor to help them gain confidence to take the next step, a mentor who had the experience in a field they were going into, or a mentor who could help them navigate entrepreneurship. Our priority was aligning people and providing *access*. We were able to match 80 out of the 110 applicants.

The big challenge in developing a mentoring relationship is chemistry. Our job was to find matches and take care of the first meetings. The rest—the chemistry—was up to them. We didn't hold anyone's hand. You're a big girl. Get to it. Once the ball is rolling, we would give them the tools to have a successful mentoring relationship. That's where I was able to come in with tips from my own mentoring experiences.

I now had a plate spinning over here for mentoring for young women in school, and I had another plate spinning over here for women later on in their careers, helping them to be successful. At the end of the first year, we conducted a survey, and out of the 80 that we matched, 100 percent said they were going to continue their mentoring relationships. Later that year I helped Jessica create the Working Women Foundation to provide micro grants to women starting their own business. Together we were truly changing the way women support one another. The need is great and I felt fortunate to have met the women I did during this time so we could all rise together.

I think back to the times when I didn't have a mentor or a kindred spirit —a capable, professional female to guide me. It feels great to know I am helping women connect with mentors by organizing mentoring programs. It also feels good knowing that I have found my tribe of women who also like to connect, empower and support one another.

Leaving the World a Better Place

I'm at the point in my career where I genuinely want to do something to give back. I helped to raise and personally give over $60 million to the Tampa Bay Community. I want to create an environment where women are working together. I want to start decreasing the competitiveness among professional women and cultivate an environment of cooperation and collaboration. In addition to my commitment to the YMCA I have invested in education institutions, mentoring programs and initiatives that speak to issues that I am passionate about.

I've started to realize, *this* is what it really looks like when you pay it forward. This is what it is all about. Yes, I have my business, and I'm passionate about it. But investing personally in my community continuines to demonstrate that I not only talk the talk but also walk the walk and be the change I want to see in the world.

As a fellow philathropist said to me, "We earn, learn, and return." I look at the path I've taken and realize I'm always learning. But you learn, you get the tools you need, and you get to work. You earn money by using what you learn, and then you return to help the next wave of women on their way up.

I do not want to be one of these people who waits until they turn 60 to start helping others and giving money away. I am not giving away millions of dollars like some of the larger philanthropists, but I am willing to put myself out there as any amount can make a difference. It's not easy, but it is a choice. If you break down the goal on a month-to-month basis, you can always give something. You don't need that much money to survive.

There is a saying: "You give your time, treasure your talent." I try to give on all levels and inspire my family and others to do the same and I challenge you to do the same.

What is your talent? Where are you putting your time? How will you invest your treasure? Figure out what is important to you, because I promise, it's worth it! And it feels good, too.

It's Time to Jump the Queue

Since starting my own consulting practice just three years ago, I have accomplished some very important goals and contributed in so many ways, including:

- Partnering with over 50 organizations in the United States to strengthen their leadership through executive

searches so we can get the right people to lead these
incredible organizations.

- Implementing numerous strategic planning sessions
  and assessments so that organizations can build
  upon growth opportunities to craft their vision for the
  future in a responsible way

- Creating fund development plans and managing
  campaigns that have raised over $15 million dollars
  to increase program capacity or build new structures
  to meet the future needs of their missions within their
  respective communities.

- Taking on four new female partners to strengthen our
  service delivery and to embody the vision that we are
  better as a collective than as an individual.

- Spearheading mentorship programs with the
  University of South Florida and Women in Leadership
  and Philanthropy so that young women have access
  to education and mentors who will help them be
  successful as they enter the workforce.

- Collaborating with Working Women of Tampa Bay to
  align entrepreneurial women with mentors as they
  look to grow our economy through the Meaningful
  Mentoring Program and provide micro grants to start
  their businesses by creating the Working Women
  Foundation.

- Providing countless hours of volunteer service to our nonprofit clients, corporate sponsorships to give back to our clients and most recently a 5-year pledge to USF to provide access for students to study abroad.

- Lastly, we have provided over 100 organizations, businesses, individuals and foundations, the necessary training and coaching to take their organization and personal growth to the next level.

I realized that my professional capacity far exceeded what I could do for one organization and the only way to create the change and legacy I wanted to see in the world was to create a new roadmap. I realized that the detractors, health challenges, and upbringing would not define my dreams and goals in life or stop me from achieving all I set out to. If it was to be it was truly up to me.

Now, I pose the question to you: What great things will you achieve? What is your roadmap? How will you pivot? What legacy will you leave behind?

We began this book with a discussion of the barriers that women face in their personal and professional lives and the new challenges facing young professional women in today's world. We've discussed the need to rise above life's circumstances and to set healthy boundaries, even when it hurts. We've discussed the value of time, the heavy toll of stress, and the importance of making your health a priority. I hope you have learned something from my stories, my successes, my trials, and my heartbreaks. Most of all, I hope this book has left you with an empowered sense of self and a better understanding of the value you can bring to this world.

With the right mentors, and with a sense of purpose and passion for what you do, no barrier will be able to stand against you. Your next step is to use the tools and strategies in this book to write your own rulebook and create your own roadmap, *now*.

There is no time like the present. Tune out the noise, rise above the detractors, and start believing in yourself—even when no one else does.

Now is your time to jump the queue. Ready or not, now is the time for you to achieve great things.

Connect with me on Facebook, Twitter or LinkedIn and share your stories about jumping the queue! Visit catalystcs.org to learn more about how I can help you or assist in connecting you with an organization so you can be the change in your community.

www.facebook.com/catalysconsultingservices

Michelle A. Turman, MA, CFRE

@MichelleATurman

About the Author

Michelle Turman, M.A., CFRE is the President of Catalyst Consulting Services whose mission is to facilitate positive change in the areas of executive searches, organizational management and fundraising. Turman received her bachelor degree from Florida State University and master's degree from University of South Florida. With over twenty-three years of nonprofit experience, Michelle has been responsible for increasing the impact and best practices of nonprofit organizations she serves and has raised over $60 million through her professional and personal philanthropic efforts.

In addition to facilitating change nationally, Michelle's community service has included leadership roles on the boards of the Arts Council of Hillsborough County, Suncoast Chapter of the Association of Fundraising Professionals, Partnership for Philanthropic Planning, Leadership Pinellas, the South Tampa YMCA, University of South Florida's Women in Leadership and Philanthropy and Working Women of Tampa Bay. In 2000, she was inducted into the prestigious Explorer's Club in New York by joining Bob Ballard, Dr. Sylvia Earle, and others for her dedication to underwater exploration and artifact conservation.

Turman is a Key Partner and educational trainer for the Nonprofit Leadership Center of Tampa Bay and at the Edyth Bush Institute for Philanthropy & Nonprofit Leadership at Rollins College. She is a Certified Fund Raising Executive and specializes in professional education in the areas of change management, capital campaigns, volunteer management, board governance, and fund development.

In 2015, Turman was recognized by Tampa Bay Metro Magazine as one of Tampa Bay's *Distinguished Women in Business* and the *Face of Nonprofit Change* in 2016 and been nominated by Tampa Bay Business Journal as *Business Woman of the Year* in 2007, 2016 and 2017.